No Holds Barred

REAL POLITICS IN AMERICA

Series Editor: Paul S. Herrnson, *University of Maryland*

The books in this series bridge the gap between academic scholarship and the popular demand for knowledge about politics. They illustrate empirically supported generalizations from original research and the academic literature using examples taken from the legislative process, executive branch decision making, court rulings, lobbying efforts, election campaigns, political movements, and other areas of American politics. The goal of the series is to convey the best contemporary political science research has to offer in ways that will engage individuals who want to know about real politics in America.

No Holds Barred:
Negativity in U.S. Senate Campaigns

Kim Fridkin Kahn
Arizona State University

Patrick J. Kenney
Arizona State University

PEARSON
Prentice
Hall

Upper Saddle River, New Jersey 07458

Library of Congress Cataloging-in-Publication Data

Kahn, Kim Fridkin.
  No holds barred: negativity in U.S. Senate campaigns/Kim Fridkin Kahn, Patrick J. Kenney.
      p. cm.—(Real politics in America)
Includes bibliographical references and index.
  ISBN 0-13-097760-8
  1. Political campaigns—United States.   2. Elections—United States.   3. United States. Congress. Senate—Elections.   I. Kenney, Patrick J.   II. Title.   III. Series.
  JK2281.K239   2004
    324.7'0973—dc22

                                                                2003015025

Editorial Director: Charlyce Jones Owen
Acquisitions Editor: Glenn Johnston
Assistant Editor: John Ragozzine
Editorial Assistant: Suzanne Remore
Director of Marketing: Beth Mejia
Marketing Assistant: Jennifer Bryant
Prepress and Manufacturing Buyer: Sherry Lewis
Interior Design: John P. Mazzola
Cover Design: Kiwi Design
Cover Photo: Ryan McVay/Getty Images, Inc.
Composition/Full-Service Project Management: Kari C. Mazzola and John P. Mazzola
Printer/Binder: RR Donnelley & Sons Company
Cover Printer: Phoenix Color Corp.

This book was set in 10/12 Palatino.

Real Politics in America
Series Editor: Paul S. Herrnson

Pearson Education LTD.
Pearson Education Singapore, Pte. Ltd
Pearson Education, Canada, Ltd
Pearson Education–Japan
Pearson Education Australia PTY, Limited

Pearson Education North Asia Ltd
Pearson Educación de Mexico, S.A. de C.V.
Pearson Education Malaysia, Pte. Ltd
Pearson Education, Upper Saddle River, NJ

10 9 8 7 6 5 4 3 2 1
ISBN 0-13-097760-8

For our parents,
Allan and Barbara Fridkin
and
Joe and Mary Jane Kenney

CONTENTS

CHAPTER 6

APPENDIX A

APPENDIX B

PREFACE

In the world of wrestling, a "no-holds-barred" fight is one in which few, if any, restrictions govern the strategies and tactics used by combatants to subdue opponents. It is nearly impossible to identify the original no-holds-barred contest. However, in 648 B.C., an athletic contest combining boxing and wrestling was introduced in the Olympics. In this contest, called the *pancratirum*, no holds were barred except biting and gouging (i.e., contestants could not thrust a finger or thumb into an opponent's eye).

No-holds-barred contests have survived for centuries. During medieval times, no-holds-barred folk football became popular. Although extremely wild and violent, the game survived well into the nineteenth century in France and Britain, where Renaissance humanist Sir Thomas Elyot condemned the game because it was more likely to injure than to benefit participants.*

No-holds-barred contests live today. Known colloquially as "ultimate fighting," contests are a combination of wrestling and boxing in which the only holds barred are biting, gouging, and punching the groin. Winners are declared when opponents either are "knocked out" or "submit" by tapping either the mat or the aggressor. Ultimate fighting is a worldwide phenomenon, generally governed by sports organizations, but sometimes not.

We consider many political campaigns to be no-holds-barred contests. In these races, there are few restrictions on the content of the campaign messages. It is not unusual for campaign messages to examine candidates' personal lives, including extra-marital affairs, prior drug use, and antiwar activities from an earlier era. Campaigns often delve into present and past financial affairs of the candidates and their families. It is difficult to imagine topics that are "barred" from discussion and debate.

---

*The information about the no-holds-barred contests of the past comes from Encyclopedia Britannica Online <www.search.eb.com>, copyright 1994–2002, Encyclopedia Britannica, Inc.

Beyond the content of campaign messages, there appear to be few restrictions on the tenor of messages in no-holds-barred contests. Candidates or surrogates, in advertisements or press releases, accuse opponents of lying, stealing, or cheating. The candidates' language, although not profane, is often accusatory, inflammatory, hyperbolic, and ad hominem. Face-to-face exchanges during debates—on television or radio—are often shrill and can be unruly and derogatory.

Approximately 40 percent of senatorial campaigns in the United States are hard-hitting contests in which, at times, virtually no holds are barred. The remaining 60 percent are low-key affairs in which incumbents hold commanding leads over inexperienced, unskilled, poorly financed challengers. Senate campaigns, then, vary from vigorous and mean-spirited contests to boring and polite blowouts. These extreme differences in the campaign climate dramatically influence the press reporting of the campaigns and the actions and attitudes of citizens.

In *No Holds Barred*, we explore the conditions that promote negative campaigning among candidates. We also examine how the tone of candidates' campaigns influences how reporters cover campaigns. Finally, we investigate how the negative information disseminated by the candidates and the press influences citizens' beliefs and behaviors. Fundamentally, we investigate how people react to no-holds-barred contests compared to mundane contests lacking any negative campaigning.

We had fun writing this book. We thank Paul Herrnson, the series editor. Paul was immediately interested in the topic. He encouraged us at each step of the process and he read and commented on every chapter. Paul was a joy to work with. We are pleased to be associated with Prentice Hall, and we are grateful to the nice people at Prentice Hall. Heather Shelstad, who was the Senior Acquisitions Editor for political science when our manuscript went into production, was very supportive of the book from its inception. Jessica Drew, Heather's editorial assistant, answered all of our questions quickly, completely, and with good cheer. Finally, we would like to thank Stacy Gordon of the University of Nevada and Robert A. Taylor of the Florida Institute of Technology for reviewing the manuscript and offering helpful suggestions.

Kim Fridkin Kahn
Patrick J. Kenney

1

AN EXPLORATION
OF NEGATIVE CAMPAIGNS

In August of 1998, a stunned nation watched as the story of President Clinton and Monica Lewinsky began to unravel. Between mid-August and Labor Day, events moved quickly. The president answered questions from a grand jury about his relationship with Monica Lewinsky. He admitted on national television that he had an "improper" relationship with Lewinsky, and he asked the nation for forgiveness, numerous times, for his actions. Clinton's detractors set a course to end his presidency. His supporters, although feeling betrayed and dismayed, believed he should finish his second term. By late August, the business of national politics seemed to stand still as the nation awaited the next chapter in this unfolding saga.

No one waited more anxiously than Democratic Senator Barbara Boxer of California.[1] She was an avid supporter of President Clinton, her daughter was married to Hillary Clinton's brother, and she was facing reelection in November. Boxer was worried that the scandal would play a role in the November elections. She feared that her opponent would criticize her, at least in part, because she supported Clinton. She was right. Matt Fong, her Republican opponent, attacked Boxer repeatedly because of her support for the president.

On the opposite coast, Republican Senator Lauch Faircloth of North Carolina viewed Clinton's admission in a completely different light. He was not, nor had he ever been, a supporter of Clinton. He felt his opposition would help him get reelected in a state that voted against Clinton for president in 1992 and 1996. He trumpeted his complaints against Clinton in his campaign and specifically linked Clinton to his Democratic opponent, John Edwards.

Although Clinton and his troubles were the basis of many negative messages in California and North Carolina in the fall of 1998, many other topics were discussed. Boxer and Faircloth, along with their opponents, spent millions of dollars delivering messages that were critical of one another. Sharp attacks were aimed at the candidates' issue positions and character traits. Harsh and uncompromising remarks were made in speeches, in press conferences, in pamphlets, and in commercials on television and radio.

These two races epitomize negative senate campaigns in contemporary America. When they occur, how the media cover them, how citizens react to them—these are the focus of this book. We intend to investigate the conditions leading candidates to criticize their opponents. We want to analyze how newspapers discuss the attacks offered by the candidates. And, maybe most importantly, we will explore how negative campaigns influence the thoughts and actions of potential voters. Our story begins with Senator Boxer's efforts to keep her seat in the U.S. Senate.

Barbara Boxer was elected to the U.S. Senate in 1992 when she defeated Bruce Herschensohn by five percentage points. Republicans in the Golden State had been eyeing her seat since the 1992 election. Elites in the Republican Party, both in California and in Washington D.C., believed she had some obvious weaknesses. Boxer failed to garner a majority of the vote in her initial election to the U.S. Senate, winning 48 percent to 43 percent. In addition, she was considered one of the most liberal members of the U.S. Senate. In fact, a liberal organization that monitors votes cast by U.S. senators reported that she supported the liberal position on every bill they monitored in 1997.[2] Maybe most telling, however, was how California voters viewed her job performance. In November of 1997, twelve months before the election, only 46 percent of Californians thought she was doing a favorable job, while 36 percent scored her job performance as unfavorable. In May of 1998, six months prior to election day, 49 percent saw her as doing a favorable job, but 40 percent viewed her job performance as unfavorable. In August, her favorable ratings were still at 49 percent, but her unfavorable scores had climbed to 43 percent.[3] In the words of campaign consultants and pollsters, her "negatives" were moving in the wrong direction, while her "positives" were frozen, still below a majority. And now, the Clinton scandal was in full bloom. Still, no rival Democrat sought the party's nomination in the June 1998 primary. She would compete for a second term. The Republicans chose Matt Fong, the current state treasurer, to unseat her.

As the Clinton scandal blitzed the airwaves in August, pollsters were busy in California trying to measure Boxer's and Fong's popularity with potential voters. A Claremont Institute poll released August 25 revealed a dead heat, 40 percent supporting Boxer and 40 percent supporting Fong, with 16 percent of the electorate undecided. The respected Field Poll, also released on August 25, found that the candidates were deadlocked, 45 percent supporting Boxer and 45 percent intending to vote for Fong, with 10 percent undecided. The Boxer/Fong campaign had all the trademarks of a hard-fought contest. The outcome was uncertain. The candidates were raising large sums of money. And, at some point, probably sooner rather than later, the candidates were going to begin pointing out their opponent's failings.

Although the candidates aired some commercials on TV in August, their campaigns began in earnest in early September. From the start, the campaign was fundamentally about matters of public policy. Boxer built her campaign around a series of issues: an improved economy, especially compared to 1992, education, gun control, the environment, and abortion. Fong, too, was interested in talking about the prominent issues of the late 1990s: health care, abortion, education, and taxes. Both the *Los Angeles Times* and the *San Francisco Chronicle*, the largest circulating newspapers in the state, spent considerable amounts of time and space examining the candidates' positions on these various topics. In total, the candidates spent over $20 million to communicate with Californians about policy matters. Boxer spent $13.7 million and Fong spent $10.7 million trying to persuade voters to support their candidacies.

Polls in early October suggested that Fong began to open a slight lead. The Field Poll released on October 8 had Fong leading by four points, 48 percent to 44 percent, with only 8 percent undecided. A *Los Angeles Times* Poll released in the first week of October had Fong ahead among "likely" voters by five points, 48 percent to 43 percent. An article in the *Los Angeles Times* on October 5 observed, "Rarely has an incumbent senator been in Democrat Barbara Boxer's shoes, entering the stretch run dead even, at best, with a challenger who began to advertise statewide only in the last few days."

Beginning in early October, the Boxer and Fong campaign strategies went in different directions. Fong stressed education more than any other issue in early October. He barely mentioned Boxer's name and he began showing ads in English, in Spanish, and in two Chinese dialects in order to widen his appeal across constituencies. On the campaign trail, Fong's approach was characterized by reporters as "low-key" and "cautious." Fong spent $3.6 million on his advertising campaign, with a great deal of that money being spent from early to mid-October. His campaign ran 2,946 30-second ads in the five major TV markets in California: Los Angeles, San Francisco/Oakland/San Jose, San Diego, Fresno, and Sacramento. Fong's ads, in the words of a *Los Angeles Times* reporter, were "blandly inoffensive." Approximately 60 percent of Fong's ads promoted his own issue positions, with the remaining 40 percent contrasting his positions with Boxer's.[4]

Boxer, on the other hand, went negative. She took aim at Fong's issue positions and attacked. She spent over $8 million on her advertising campaign, more than doubling Fong's spending. She aired 5,812 commercials in the big five TV markets in California, nearly doubling Fong. Approximately 20 percent of Boxer's ads promoted her positions, while 45 percent exclusively attacked Fong's positions, and the remaining 35 percent drew sharp contrasts between her positions and Fong's. *Los Angeles Times* reporters described Boxer's strategy as "opening both barrels at state Treasurer Fong." Writers noted that she employed "a series of hard-hitting, and largely unanswered, TV commercials targeting Fong's stance on gun control, abortion, and HMO reforms."

In mid-October, Boxer and Fong went back and forth on the abortion issue. The content and tone of their ads on abortion capture nicely their different strategies. Boxer initiated the assault with a commercial on abortion, titled "Who Decides." It contained strong language linking Fong to conservative and controversial House Speaker Republican Newt Gingrich.

> Narrator: Since 1993, extremists in Congress have tried over 100 times to restrict a women's right to choose. Now they're behind senate candidate Matt Fong's campaign. Matt Fong is not pro-choice. He thinks government should decide. That's why we need to keep Barbara Boxer in the Senate. She's led the fight to protect our right to choose.
>
> Boxer then appears: I'll always stand up for a women's right to choose. We simply can't go back to the days when government told women what to do.
>
> Narrator: Senator Barbara Boxer. The right direction for California.

As the narrator is talking about "extremists in Congress," there is a picture of Speaker Newt Gingrich speaking at a fundraiser for Matt Fong. The ad expressly states that Gingrich and Fong are extremists on the issue of abortion.

Fong's ad, titled "Abortion," was less confrontational. He talks poignantly about his mother's decision to place Fong up for adoption.

> Fong: I was adopted from an orphanage when I was five months old. My birth mother's choice gave me the chance to be part of a loving family. My opponent says I oppose a woman's right to choose. She is not telling the truth. I respect a woman's right to choose in the first trimester. Unlike my opponent, I oppose indiscriminate late-term abortions. I believe in parental consent, and I strongly support making adoptions easier and less expensive.

Boxer launched similar ads on the issues of gun control and the environment. In addition, the Democratic Party moved into the fray and aired 681 ads in the five main media markets in California, all negative, all attacking Fong on his issue positions. Similar to the Boxer advertisement on abortion, the Democratic Party struck first on the issue of HMO reform. The Democratic Party ad accused Fong of opposing legislation that would allow HMOs to be sued by their members for poor quality medical care. Fong, once again, answered the advertisement with an explanation of his position and an assertion that Boxer was distorting his stance. The elite media in California began directing their attention at Boxer's onslaught. For example, a headline in the *San Francisco Chronicle* on October 17 read, "Boxer's Allies Take Tough Line on Fong in New TV Ads." For approximately two weeks in mid-October, Fong only reacted to Boxer's charges. Fong's hesitancy to take the initiative allowed Boxer to set the campaign agenda.

Polls in late October indicated that Fong's lead had disappeared and he was actually falling behind. The *Los Angeles Times* Poll released on October 23 found Boxer leading by five percentage points, 49 percent to 44 percent, with 7 percent undecided. The Field Poll, released on October 28, indicated that Boxer had increased her lead to 51 percent to 42 percent, with 7 percent still undecided. As the month of October ended, Boxer's campaign put together one more round of negative ads to be aired during the first few days of November.

In the face of falling polling numbers, Fong scrambled and decided to take the offensive. He attacked Boxer on three fronts: her ideology, her personality, and her support of Clinton during the Lewinsky affair. He produced and ran ads claiming Boxer was "too liberal and too ineffective for California." His rhetoric on the campaign trail also changed. Campaigning in Orange County in the last week of October he asserted, "She is a left-wing radical. She has a resume filled with votes that have made life tougher for working families and senior citizens, with tax increase after tax increase."

Fong also took aim at Boxer's personality, characterizing her as "divisive," "polarizing," and "sometimes caustic." He stressed that her unbending and uncompromising personal nature made it difficult for her to work with Republicans in order to do what is best for California and the nation. At a fund-raiser for Fong, Senator Bob Dole claimed that "Boxer was nearly the most obstinate Democrat he had ever met."

Lastly, in the eleventh hour, Fong focused criticisms on her support of Clinton. He stressed that she made many public comments concerning sexual allegations that involved Robert Packwood, a Republican senator from Oregon, and Clarence Thomas, a Republican appointee to the Supreme Court. In both cases she passionately supported the women as they battled politically powerful men. Now, although she was mostly silent on the Clinton affair, when she spoke, she stood by Clinton. Fong claimed, "The issue isn't Monica Lewinsky, it's Barbara Boxer's double standard. She has one standard for her friends and another for Republicans."

The state's journalists were quick to notice the change of tactics. The headline in an article appearing in the *San Francisco Chronicle* on October 30 read, "Fong Ads Switch to Attack Mode." And the subheading read, "He abandons nice-guy tactics, rips into Boxer as poll standing slumps." The reporter, John Wildermuth, wrote, "The new ad (calling Boxer too liberal) is a complete reversal for Fong, whose television campaign until now has featured him strolling through idyllic groves of redwoods and speaking earnestly into the camera on purposely noncontroversial issues. It follows a complete reversal in Fong's poll numbers, which have seen him go from four points up to nine points down in just three weeks. Over the same period, Fong's studied, low-key approach has been effectively bludgeoned by Boxer's unending stream of negative ads."

Election day arrived with both Boxer and Fong running negative ads across the state. By early evening it was apparent that Boxer was going to win. She won by more than 10 percent, defeating Fong 53 percent to 43 percent. The 53 percent victory was nearly 15 percent higher than her support at the polls in late August and 10 percent higher than her support in late September. Why the turnabout?

Campaign strategists, the California media, and even academics offered explanations. Their discussions centered primarily on one thing: Boxer's negative ads. Experts agreed that the ads brought about two effects that changed the landscape of the campaign. First, Boxer's ads actually persuaded citizens to move away from Fong and support Boxer. That is, the ads shaped the information voters used when they evaluated the strengths and weaknesses of the competing candidates. And, second, by identifying Fong's issue positions, Boxer's ads mobilized traditional Democratic partisans to vote on election day in order to keep Fong from serving in the U.S. Senate.

Campaign consultants were quick to point to Boxer's attacks as shaping voters' opinions. Democratic strategist and former press secretary to President Clinton, Dee Dee Meyers, explained that Boxer's ads were effective at identifying why Fong was on the wrong side of issues that were salient to many California voters. A similar analysis emanated from the GOP. Dan Schnur, a GOP consultant, noted, "The race is a reminder to Republicans that if we don't define the issues, the other side will. Once you decide to fight on the other side's issues, you've already lost."

Media analyses from the *Los Angeles Times* and *San Francisco Chronicle* agreed that Boxer's attacks persuaded voters to stay away from Fong. Mark Barabak, the *Los Angeles Times* political writer, contended "The Democrat evidently reversed her position in the see-saw contest through a series of hard-hitting . . . TV commercials. Boxer's surge between September and October demonstrates anew the potency—indeed, primacy—of television advertising in California politics." Susan Pinkus, the director of the *Los Angeles Times* poll, believed, "She [Boxer] succeeded in turning the race away from a straight referendum on her incumbency, which Fong wanted, into more of an issue-focused contest between the two candidates." John Wildermuth, the *Chronicle* political writer, stressed, "Down in the polls and written off by Republicans and Democrats alike just weeks before the election, Boxer used a $9 million arsenal of attack ads to roll over Fong and win by a more-than-comfortable 10-point margin. Boxer used those issues [abortion, gun control, environmental regulation, HMO reform] as the centerpiece of a nastily effective campaign of negative ads slamming Fong as an extremist for his more conservative positions."

Professor Bruce Cain, a professor of political science at the University of California at Berkeley, also argued that Boxer was able to convince voters that Fong was on the wrong side of several key issues in California politics. Cain notes in an article in the *Chronicle* on October 30, "It's obvious that Boxer has done what she had to do and defined Matt Fong in relation to the issues. The question is why Fong didn't start screaming earlier that Boxer was a liberal."

Beyond shaping the criteria voters used to assess Fong and Boxer, Boxer's ads may have also motivated traditional Democratic supporters to get to the polls on election day. Boxer's campaign strategists were worried about low turnout in 1998. They had good reasons to be concerned. Boxer's first election was during the presidential election year of 1992 when approximately 46 percent of potential voters cast ballots in the senatorial election. But, in the off-year senatorial election of 1994, between Dianne Feinstein and Michael

Huffington, only 33 percent of eligible voters came to the polls. Could Boxer win in an off-year election? She stressed frequently on the campaign trail, "Guess what: If everyone votes, we win."

The Boxer strategists took aim at systematically increasing turnout among Democrats. Boxer's campaign manager, Rose Kaploczynski, noted in an interview that Boxer's campaign approached the "turnout question" from two angles. First, Boxer employed traditional methods of increasing support among key partisans, such as phone calls, rides to the polls, and sending volunteers door to door to remind Democrats to vote. But, second, Kaploczynski hoped that the harsh critiques of Fong's issue positions would encourage traditional Democrats to "get to the polls." The idea here is that harsh attacks identify key reasons to support your party's nominee, while identifying potential risks for supporting the opponent. Kaploczynski's strategy may have worked. Turnout on election day 1998 was 35 percent of the eligible electorate, a full half-million votes higher than the 1994 off-year election.

In the end, there is a clear consensus among political strategists, media experts, and even academics that Boxer's negative commercials were the key to her victory. Boxer's campaign strategy and ultimate victory exemplify why campaign consultants and political candidates employ negative messages in ads and on the campaign trail.

While the Boxer strategists demonstrated the effectiveness of the attack strategy on the West Coast, 3,000 miles to the east in the heart of tobacco country, Republican Senator Lauch Faircloth from North Carolina launched his own negative campaign against Democratic challenger John Edwards. Faircloth, like Boxer, was completing his first term as a U.S. senator in the fall of 1998. He faced no opposition in the Republican primary, but the winner of the Democratic primary, John Edwards, appeared formidable. He was wealthy, he was much younger than the 70-year-old Faircloth, and he was articulate when he discussed his issue agenda, both on the campaign trail and on TV. He stressed a package of issues including Social Security, medicare, a patient bill of rights, education, and the environment.

Faircloth's initial victory in the Senate six years earlier was not overwhelming. Faircloth defeated incumbent Senator Terry Sanford by a margin of 50 percent to 46 percent. During Faircloth's first campaign, Sanford stopped campaigning for more than two weeks in October of 1992 to have heart valve replacement surgery and was unable to campaign rigorously for much of October. Given Faircloth's less than stellar victory in 1992, Democrats viewed him as vulnerable. To deflect criticisms that Faircloth came to office while the incumbent slept, literally, Faircloth worked hard to establish a strong following in North Carolina in the mid-1990s. Faircloth was a loyal Republican in the Senate, he worked hard with Senator Jesse Helms, North Carolina's senior senator, to bring goods and services to the Tar Heel state, and he criticized President Clinton frequently and sharply on policy and personal grounds. He was diligent in his efforts to assist constituents; yet he was remarkably out-of-sight compared to his flamboyant companion, Helms. The citizens' views of his performance reflected his efforts and style. In March of 1998, eight months before election day, 45 percent of North Carolinians rated him as doing a favorable job, only 17 percent scored him unfavorably, while a whopping 40 percent did not rate him at all. These numbers were essentially unchanged in July of 1998: 45 percent favorable, 22 percent unfavorable, and 30 percent with no opinion.

Faircloth spent the late summer of 1998 criticizing Clinton for his actions with Monica Lewinsky. He was outraged at Clinton's behavior and, on numerous occasions, Faircloth condemned the president's actions. As Faircloth's campaign began in earnest, he shifted his criticisms from Clinton to Edwards. To be sure, Faircloth reminded voters that he was a "common sense" Republican, who was loyal to North Carolina, and who worked hard to help all constituents. Faircloth also stressed that he was a successful hog farmer who had run a successful business and "had never missed a payroll." But the thrust of his message early in the campaign was negative. Faircloth's criticisms were aimed primarily at two topics: Edward's background and Edward's connections with Clinton.

A Mason-Dixon poll taken in mid-September showed Faircloth was leading Edwards, 50 percent to 40 percent, with only 10 percent undecided. In the wake of these polling numbers, Faircloth ran two critical ads. One 30-second ad accused Edwards, a highly successful personal-injury lawyer, of "the lawyer's habit of stretching the truth." The commercial emphasized Edwards's promise not to accept money from political action committees (PACs), but discussed Edwards's acceptance of $679,000 from individual trial lawyers. The second ad accused Edwards of misleading voters about his place of birth. Edwards claimed in literature and on the campaign trail that he grew up in Robbins, North Carolina. Faircloth's advertisement pointed out, however, that Edwards had moved from Senaca, South Carolina, to Robbins when Edwards was twelve years old. Chuck Fuller, a spokesperson for Faircloth's campaign, was quoted in the *Herald-Sun*, the largest circulating paper in Durham, North Carolina, stressing that, "Since John Edwards won't tell the truth about his background and liberal past, we will."

Edwards countered with a two-fold response. He repeated his call to end all TV advertising and replace the ads with several debates across the state covering a wide range of issues. Edwards began this theme early, in late summer. He ran a commercial in late September restating his position. In Edwards's words, "I want to debate face to face. He makes his case; I make mine. Senator Faircloth just runs negative ads. I think you deserve better." Faircloth, as he did throughout the campaign, refused to debate.

In addition, Edwards stayed focused on the issues. He dedicated each week to an issue theme. For example, during the week of September 21 he introduced his ideas on health care. He discussed his positions in a series of town meetings across North Carolina. One meeting was in Greensboro, North

Carolina, and the local paper, *News and Record,* ran a headline on September 24, "Edwards Pitches Health Care Reform in Visit." The sub-headline stressed, "U.S. Senate Candidate John Edwards Makes the Two Must-Visit for Politicians Campaigning in Greensboro: Rotary Club and Robinson's Restaurant."

A Mason-Dixon poll conducted in early October showed Faircloth's lead had narrowed, 45 percent intending to vote for Faircloth, 43 percent intending to vote for Edwards, and 12 percent undecided. The race was a "dead heat." Faircloth continued his attack against Edwards but he shifted topics. Faircloth began to link Edwards to Clinton. Faircloth linked the two Democrats in several ways. First, he found a financial connection. Clinton had come to North Carolina to raise money for Edwards. Faircloth's critique, "He (Clinton) came down here to raise $400,000 for John Edwards. Why? Because Bill Clinton wants a liberal senator he can control." Second, he linked Clinton and Edwards on the highly contentious issue of the tobacco tax. Faircloth's claim, "Edwards is a 'Clinton Clone' and he will join the President in increasing the tax on tobacco." Finally, he drew connections on the possibility of impeachment. Faircloth argued that Clinton could count on Edwards's support if an impeachment vote came to the forefront. In sharp contrast, Faircloth, at a rally in Asheville, North Carolina, stated his own position, "I believe he (Clinton) has got me on the doubtful list."

Faircloth's negative attacks were ubiquitous. He spent $9,370,462 on his campaign, with over half of the expenditures aimed exclusively at producing and airing his commercials. Faircloth aired 9,910 ads in the three largest media-market areas: Raleigh-Durham, Charlotte, and Greensboro. Well over 50 percent of his 30-second commercials were exclusively negative. The remaining ads simply promoted Faircloth as a U.S. senator and stressed his hard work on behalf of the residents of North Carolina. The Republican Party, too, spent nearly $300,000 on the production and airing of ads, all of which were negative. The GOP aired 745 negative spots in the Raleigh-Durham, Charlotte, and Greensboro areas. The commercials by the Republican Party echoed the themes that Faircloth was emphasizing.[5]

In mid-to-late October, Edwards's own ads remained primarily focused on the issues. Edwards's ads called for hiring teachers, for building schools, for fixing Social Security. Edwards also continued to recommend a patients' bill of rights for citizens using HMOs. The ad campaign was often coordinated with Edwards's stump speeches. If he was talking about Social Security, then ads appeared on TV about Social Security. Edwards's ads ran in the same media markets as Faircloth's: Raleigh-Durham, Charlotte, and Greensboro. Edwards spent over $8 million to unseat Faircloth, with over half of the money spent on airing 30-second ads. He ran 8,870 spots in the big three markets, and less than 5 percent of these ads were exclusively negative. A whopping 65 percent of the spots stressed Edwards's positions on his key issues. To be sure, ads crossed the airwaves that were critical of Faircloth, but these ads were produced and run by the Democratic Party. In fact, the Democratic Party spent over $800,000 on the production and airing of ads, translating into 1,446 spots in the Raleigh-Durham, Charlotte, and Greensboro areas, twice the GOP effort. All of the Democratic Party's ads were negative, every one. The ads were aimed primarily at Faircloth's record in the Senate. For example, ads paid for by the North Carolina Democratic Party criticized Faircloth for voting to cut hundreds of millions of dollars for Medicare and for missing votes on the Senate floor. The ads did not mention Edwards by name. And, when asked about the ads, Edwards's campaign stressed, "He has no control over them since they are not produced by his campaign."

On October 30 a headline in the *Winston-Salem Journal* read, "Poll Shows Candidates Neck-and-Neck as Election Nears." The paper reported a Mason-Dixon Poll that indicated 44 percent of likely voters intended to vote for Faircloth, 43 percent of likely voters said they were going to support Edwards, while 13 percent remained undecided. In the last week of the campaign the candidates raced across North Carolina and blitzed TV sets with 30-second ads. On the last day of the campaign Faircloth flew across the state, stopping frequently to talk to loyal supporters. All the while, his ads continued to criticize Edwards. On the final weekend of the campaign, Edwards again challenged Faircloth to withdraw his ads and enter into a debate. At the University of North Carolina at Charlotte, Edwards repeated his position, "What do you see when you turn on your TV these days? A lot of hateful, 30-second personal attacks. What you see on TV can make you sick to your stomach. We need to appear together. We should answer questions from a group of voters. They're entitled to it." Faircloth answered quickly that he would not debate, and he stated firmly that the Democratic Party of North Carolina was responsible for many of the negative ads appearing on television.

Although the polls suggested neither candidate had an advantage, on election day the voters chose Edwards. Edwards defeated Faircloth 51 percent to 47 percent. Faircloth dropped approximately 15 points in the polls between early September and election day. Why the turnabout?

Similar to the Boxer/Fong race, campaign strategists, the North Carolina media, and academics offered explanations. Their discussions centered primarily on one thing: Faircloth's negative ads. Yet, in contrast to California where pundits believed Boxer's negative ads propelled her to a second term in the U.S. Senate, the experts in North Carolina believed Faircloth's negative attacks cost him his seat in the U.S. Senate. Consultants, reporters, and professors agreed that Faircloth's ads actually persuaded people to move away from Faircloth to Edwards. And Faircloth's attacks on Edwards, by way of Clinton, galvanized higher turnout among traditional Democratic constituencies, especially among black voters, who constitute approximately one-fifth of the voting age population in North Carolina.

Analysts believed that Faircloth's dual aim of attacking Edwards directly and linking Edwards to Clinton had two separate effects. First, the frontal assaults on Edwards's character and his background in late September, known as the "blow it up" ads within the Faircloth camp, actually cost Faircloth points in the polls in early October. Faircloth's campaign manager, Chuck Fuller, commenting in an Associated Press story appearing in several newspapers across North Carolina regretted the "blow it up" strategy. He admitted there was a "bitter internal dispute" during the campaign about how to attack Edwards. But, in the end, "implying that Edwards was a lying lawyer" may have hurt Faircloth's level of support. The Voter News Service polling group completed an exit survey of over 1,500 voters on election day and released the results to the Associated Press and the major television networks. AP writer Emery Dalesio summarized the exit poll results, "Many voters said the Republican's ads backfired." The attacks focusing on Edwards's profession were seen as irrelevant by voters.

Faircloth's second wave of attacks aimed at Edwards and Clinton were particularly harmful to his efforts. Indeed, many commentators thought that these ads were the key to Edwards's victory. Strategists, exit polls, and academics believe that the critiques of Clinton actually mobilized traditional Democratic voters to go to the polls. A headline in an Associated Press story read, "Black Turnout, Soft GOP, Key Edwards Win." Faircloth's campaign manager, Chuck Fuller, believed turnout was the key, "This was a turnout election. This was about who went to vote. Obviously, the Democrats did a better job turning out their core vote." Typically, in North Carolina, black Americans comprise 15 percent of the electorate, but in the Faircloth/Edwards race blacks made up 20 percent of the electorate. In North Carolina, as in the rest of the nation, over 90 percent of black Americans voted Democratic, in this case for Edwards.

Why was turnout higher among the Democratic Party's most loyal supporters? Political science professors Ted Arrington and Thad Beyle hypothesize that Faircloth's attacks on Clinton motivated black citizens to vote. Arrington explains, "Black turnout made the difference. I interpret that to mean that they believed President Clinton was threatened by the Republicans, and they interpreted that to mean that they were threatened." Beyle expands on Arrington's explanation, "Black voters have not felt as connected to a president since Lyndon Johnson. I spent three hours in a black church in Washington on Sunday, the message got out, despite [the] not-so-good weather."

Lastly, juxtaposed with Faircloth's attacks was Edwards's decision to remain focused on his issue priorities. Evidence from exit polls indicated that voters were most concerned about Social Security and health care in North Carolina, two of the issues Edwards spent a great deal of time talking about. John Davis, executive director of *North Carolina FREE*, a business-sponsored political research group, believed that Edwards's decision to talk about key issues, while Faircloth focused on the negative, was the key to his victory. Davis's analysis was that, "The agenda of the year never really changed from health care and Social Security. The national Republican leaders blundered by launching a last-minute, television blitz linking a disgraced Clinton to Democratic congressional candidates."

The similarities between the campaigns in California and North Carolina were dramatic. Both campaigns involved one-term incumbents seeking reelection; both campaigns were held in populous states; both campaigns were held in the same year; both campaigns were expensive; both campaigns produced and employed extensive amounts of 30-second TV commercials; both campaigns saw the Republican and Democratic parties air a large number of negative ads; and in both campaigns, incumbents initiated negative campaign messages aimed at their opponents. Yet the outcomes were vastly different. One incumbent won easily and the other lost decisively.

The elections in California and North Carolina illustrate the on-going and unsettled debate concerning the impact of negative campaigns. The intended effects of negative campaigning are difficult to predict. Why did negative campaigning assist Boxer, yet hamper Faircloth's reelection? In this book, we intend to answer this question by exploring the dynamics of negative campaigns. Under what circumstances do candidates decide to "go negative?" What negative campaign messages do the media decide to cover and disseminate to the public? Do negative campaigns affect the likelihood that citizens go to the polls? Do negative messages alter how potential voters evaluate candidates?

These questions cannot be answered by looking only at the campaigns in California and North Carolina. These races are illustrative, but they cannot provide definitive answers. In fact, the two races provoke more questions than answers. For example, why did both incumbents initiate the attacks during their respective campaigns? Boxer was behind in the polls and Faircloth was ahead. Why did Boxer gain in the polls while Faircloth dropped in the polls after both incumbents attacked in late September? Why were newspapers in California perplexed that Fong did not counterattack sooner, while newspapers in North Carolina found Edwards's decision not to attack Faircloth refreshing? Why did the negative attacks increase turnout for the Democrats in both races? After all, Faircloth's attacks on Edwards mobilized Democratic turnout every bit as well as Boxer's assaults on Fong.

To understand the nature and consequences of negative campaigns, we must explore dozens of campaigns, not just a couple. We need to look at many and varied candidate strategies. We need to investigate the press accounts of campaigns across the country. And, maybe most importantly, we need to see the reactions of voters in races with varying degrees of negativity. We describe our examination of campaign strategies, news media coverage, and voters' impressions of senate candidates in the next section.

DESIGN AND DATA

To examine the conduct and impact of negativity in campaigns, we concentrate on U.S. Senate campaigns. U.S. Senate elections are an ideal laboratory for examining the impact of negative messages because these campaigns vary dramatically in terms of candidate messages, media coverage, and voters' views of the candidates. Furthermore, the level of competition varies sharply from one senate campaign to another. In this book, we examine the population of senate races for an entire election cycle. In particular, we look at 97 contested races between 1988 and 1992. In addition, we update the 1988–1992 senate races with the examination of more recent campaigns, primarily senate campaigns contested in 1998.

MEASURING THE TONE OF THE CANDIDATES' CAMPAIGNS

In our inquiry we examine the candidates' choice of campaign strategies. In particular, we examine the conditions influencing a candidate's decision to "go negative." We employ three distinct datasets to measure the tone of the candidates' campaigns.

INTERVIEWING CAMPAIGN MANAGERS

To measure the tone of the candidates' campaigns, we relied on several sources of information. First, we conducted telephone interviews with the campaign managers of the major party candidates running for election to the U.S. Senate in 1988, 1990, and 1992. With 97 contested races, the population of managers consisted of 194 managers (i.e., one for each candidate). These surveys were conducted between November, 1991, and June, 1993. Interviews were completed with 147 of the 194 campaign managers, yielding a response rate of 76 percent.[6]

In addition, we build on this cross-sectional dataset of campaign managers by creating a panel of senators running for election in 1992 and 1998. In particular, in 1992, we interviewed campaign managers for 27 of the 33 candidates who won election to the U.S. Senate. Twenty of these senators decided to run for reelection in 1998. Of the twenty "eligible" senators, we completed interviews with nineteen of the campaign offices, for a response rate in 1998 of 95 percent. The survey questionnaire in 1998 mirrors the earlier interview schedule, allowing for comparisons across the two election years.[7]

CONTENT ANALYSES OF CANDIDATES' ADVERTISEMENTS FROM 1988 TO 1992

We also examined the content of the candidates' political advertisements. We examined televised political advertisements, since these commercials are a central component of U.S. Senate campaigns.[8] We relied on the Political Commercial Archive at the University of Oklahoma to obtain our sample of political commercials.[9]

The number of advertisements available for the candidates varied widely since some candidates produced considerably more ads than other candidates.

We randomly selected four advertisements for each of the candidates running for the U.S. Senate in 1988, 1990, and 1992. Our sample includes 594 ads from 161 candidates.

For each commercial, we coded the overall message of the ad; specific discussions of issues, ideology, and traits; as well as the tone of the ads. We assessed the tone of the advertisement in three ways. First, each ad received an overall score that was either positive, negative, or a combination of the two. Second, any negative discussion of issues or traits was recorded. Third, we counted the number of criticisms that appeared in the commercial.[10]

CONTENT ANALYSES OF CANDIDATES' ADVERTISEMENTS IN 1998

To update our political advertising data, we relied on data available through the Brennan Institute of Justice at their Web site <buyingtime.org>. The Brennan Institute has made advertisements collected by Campaign Media Analysis Group (CMAG) available. CMAG, a commercial firm, monitors political advertising by the major television networks and twenty-five leading cable networks in seventy-five media markets. These seventy-five media markets reach over 80 percent of the population. Students from Arizona State University used a coding instrument to evaluate the content of each ad, rating tone, issue content, use of party labels, and whether an ad urged a specific action.[11] In total, over 24,000 advertisements were coded for the population of U.S. Senate contests in 1998.

THE NEWS MEDIA'S COVERAGE OF THE CAMPAIGN

During campaigns, voters receive the bulk of their information about candidates from the news media. Also, given the primacy of the news media, we were interested in examining how the tone of the candidates' messages influences news media coverage of the campaign. We conducted an extensive content analysis of press coverage in each state holding a senate election in 1988, 1990, and 1992.

We selected the largest circulating newspaper in each state for analysis simply because more potential voters read these newspapers. Newspapers, instead of television news, were chosen to represent news coverage because newspapers allocate more resources and more space to their coverage of statewide campaigns and people depend on local newspapers more than local television news for information about senatorial campaigns.[12]

News coverage was examined between September 1 and election day.[13] We examined all articles that mentioned either candidate in the first section, state section, and editorial section of the newspaper.[14] In total, 6,925 articles were coded for the population of senate elections.

In conducting the content analysis of media coverage, we wanted to capture how the media portrayed the race to voters. We also wanted to measure how closely the news coverage mirrored the candidates' messages. We matched the content analysis of the newspapers with the content analysis of the candidates' commercials. We coded the amount, tone, and substance of issue and trait discussion in the news. For example, we assessed the overall tone of all headlines and articles. In addition, we recorded the number and source of criticisms. We also measured the content of the criticisms.[15]

MEASURING CITIZENS' VIEWS OF THE SENATE CANDIDATES

To study how the negativity of the campaign influences the attitudes and actions of potential voters, we relied on the National Election Study (NES) Senate Election Study (SES). The NES/SES was designed specifically to study senate elections since it includes (roughly) equal numbers of respondents from all fifty states.[16]

With these data, we can see if the tone of the campaign influences respondents' general awareness of the campaign. For example, there are questions focusing on a respondent's exposure to the senate candidates. There are also questions concentrating on whether respondents pay attention to the campaign via the media. The NES/SES also includes questions that allow us to examine how the tone of the campaign affects citizens' evaluations of candidates. For example, the dataset includes questions measuring general evaluations of the candidates using "feeling thermometers," questions about respondents' vote decisions, as well as questions assessing the respondents' "likes" and "dislikes" about the candidates. In addition, the NES/SES asks respondents whether they voted in the senate election. Finally, the interviews include a number of political (e.g., party identification) and demographic questions (e.g., age, income) about the respondents. By combining the NES/SES data with information about the tone of the candidates' campaigns and patterns of news coverage, we can examine how the negativity of the campaign influences citizens' assessments of the competing candidates as well as citizens' likelihood of participating in the election.

THE PLAN OF THE BOOK

Chapter 2 explores the question: When do candidates go negative? In this chapter we identify the circumstances leading candidates to launch negative attacks on opponents. The theme that emerges is that candidates' decisions are far from random. They initiate negative messages under specific conditions. In particular, competition breeds negativity by both incumbents and challengers. When the outcome of the race is uncertain, candidates work hard to criticize opponents on a range of dimensions, such as issue agendas, issue positions, and personal characteristics. Also, incumbents and challengers save the brunt of their attacks for the final weeks of campaigns. Not surprisingly, candidates want voters to have reasons to reject opponents "at their fingertips" on election day.

Although incumbents and challengers are both more likely to "go negative" in close races and late in campaigns, there are differences in the campaign strategies of incumbents and challengers. For example, incumbents avoid negative appeals altogether if they are safely ahead in the polls. Challengers, on the other hand, are much more likely to attack even in relatively hopeless contests. The content of incumbents' attacks tends to focus on challengers' issue agendas and positions. Challengers work hard to link incumbents to failed public policies and to the negative aspects of the "Washington Establishment" (e.g., corporate campaign contributions). Finally, in Chapter 2 we compare the negative strategies used by male and female senatorial candidates. We find men are more likely than women to rely on negative campaign appeals. Furthermore, when choosing between a positive and negative campaign strategy, men are more responsive than women to the campaign environment (e.g., the closeness of the race).

Chapter 3 examines the question: When does the press go negative? We describe the patterns of negative press coverage in local newspapers. Negative messages appear throughout newspapers; critical commentary about the candidates' issue stands, personal traits, and poll standings are sprinkled in headlines and throughout articles. The likelihood of negative coverage changes in response to levels of competition and candidates' strategies. Competition consistently affects press criticisms. However, competition influences coverage differently for incumbents and challengers. For incumbents, as races become more hard-fought, press coverage becomes more negative. For challengers, media coverage does not always become more critical in close races. In fact, for certain types of news content, competitive challengers receive more favorable coverage than noncompetitive challengers.

In Chapter 3, we also examine the press's use of "ad watches." Ad watches became popular in the news media in the 1990s and examine the veracity of the information presented in the candidates' commercials. Editors and reporters find that the accuracy of candidates' ads decreases in competitive campaigns and when candidates rely on negative commercials. We discuss the utility of this kind of coverage for a distracted electorate trying to sort through the competing claims of dueling candidates.

Chapter 4 examines the question: Do negative campaigns inform citizens? In this chapter we discuss the importance of distinguishing between different types of negative messages. The first type of negative message is presented in a legitimate fashion and focuses on topics relevant to governing. The second type of negative message, "mudslinging," is characterized by irrelevant and shrill attacks. We discover that both types of negative messages increase voters' knowledge about the candidates and the campaign. For example, when the candidates' advertisements become more negative and when candidates sling mud at each other, citizens are more likely to correctly identify the candidates' campaign themes. While the results in Chapter 4 demonstrate the benefits of both types of negative messages, the costs associated with mudslinging become clear in Chapter 5.

Chapter 5 explores the complex question: Do negative campaigns influence the beliefs and behaviors of citizens? We examine how negative campaigns influence (1) citizens' levels of interest in campaigns; (2) citizens' likelihood of going to the polls; and (3) citizens' evaluations of competing candidates. We find that mudslinging has a deleterious effect on citizens' attitudes and actions. When campaigns are filled with harsh attacks on irrelevant topics, voters are less interested in campaigns, they develop less positive impressions of the candidates, and they are more likely to stay home on election day. Indeed, mudslinging shrinks the size of the electorate and makes it more elite, more affluent, and more partisan.

However, not all negative messages have harmful effects. In particular, critical commentary, presented in a legitimate fashion on appropriate topics, can favorably influence citizens' views and actions. For example, as the proportion of criticisms in the press increase, citizens become more interested in campaigns and are more likely to participate in elections.

In addition, and as expected, negative commercials lead people to develop more critical impressions of the candidate targeted in the "attack" ads. However, candidates—especially incumbents—suffer a backlash when they attack their opponents. In particular, when incumbents air more negative commercials, citizens develop less favorable impressions of these incumbents.

Chapter 6 compares the key findings of the book with the conventional wisdom regarding negative campaigning in the United States. We point out the conflicting views held by politicians, pundits, the press, and citizens concerning negative campaigns. We suggest specific revisions to these views by explaining how inconsistencies about the value of negative campaigning can be reconciled. The findings in this book, derived from analyses of nearly one hundred U.S. Senate campaigns, will help students of American politics understand the nature and consequences of negative campaigns at the birth of the twenty first century.

NOTES

1. For another description of the Boxer-Fong campaign, see Michael A. Bailey, "So Close and Yet So Far," in *Campaign and Elections: Contemporary Case Studies*, ed. Michael A. Bailey, Ronald A. Faucheux, Paul S. Herrnson, and Clyde Wilcox (Washington, D.C.: Congressional Quarterly Press, 2000).
2. Americans for Democratic Action (ADA) monitors a broad spectrum of votes by members of Congress. A perfect liberal score is 100. Boxer received 100 in 1997 and 95 in 1998.

3. The surveys inquiring about favorable/unfavorable ratings were conducted by the Field Poll in California.

4. Information about the candidates' advertisements comes from Jonathan S. Krasno and Daniel E. Seltz, *Buying Time: Television Advertising in the 1998 Congressional Elections* (New York: Brennan Center for Justice at New York University School of Law, 2000).

5. Information about the candidates' advertisements comes from Jonathan S. Krasno and Daniel E. Seltz, *Buying Time: Television Advertising in the 1998 Congressional Elections.*

6. The response rate is nearly identical for the three election years: 73 percent for managers of 1988 campaigns, 79 percent for managers of 1990 campaigns, and 72 percent for managers of 1992 campaigns. The interviews averaged twenty-two minutes in length, with the shortest interview ten minutes and the longest interview forty-five minutes. See Kim Fridkin Kahn and Patrick J. Kenney, *The Spectacle of U.S. Senate Campaigns* (Princeton, NJ: Princeton University Press, 1999) for more details about the campaign manager interviews.

7. See Kim Fridkin Kahn and Patrick J. Kenney, "The Dynamics of Senate Campaign Messages," paper presented at the annual meeting of the American Political Science Association, Washington, D.C., 2000, for more information about the panel survey.

8. See Steven Ansolabehere, Roy Behr, and Shanto Iyengar, *The Media Game: American Politics in the Television Age* (New York: Macmillan Publishing Company, 1993); Edie N. Goldenberg and Michael W. Traugott, *Campaigning for Congress* (Washington, D.C.: Congressional Quarterly Press, 1984); Frank I. Luntz, *Candidates Consultants and Campaigns: The Style and Substance of American Electioneering* (Oxford: Basil Blackwell, Ltd., 1988).

9. The Archive has the largest collection of U.S. Senate advertisements publicly available for this time period.

10. Three coders were sent to the Archive in Oklahoma. Intercoder reliability among our coders averaged 88 percent across the ads.

11. For more information about the Brennan Institute data, see Jonathan S. Krasno and Daniel E. Seltz, *Buying Time: Television Advertising in the 1998 Congressional Elections* (New York: Brennan Center for Justice at New York University School of Law, 2000).

12. Kim Fridkin Kahn and Patrick J. Kenney, *The Spectacle of U.S. Senate Campaigns* (Princeton, NJ: Princeton University Press, 1999); Mary Ellen Leary, *Phantom Politics: Campaigning in California* (Washington, D.C.: Public Affairs Press, 1977); William G. Mayer, "Trends: Trends in Media Usage," *Public Opinion Quarterly* 57 (1993): 593–611; Mark C. Westlye, *Senate Elections and Campaign Intensity* (Baltimore, MD: Johns Hopkins University Press, 1991).

13. In those cases where the state's primary election was held after September 1, coding began the day after the primary. We examined every other day from September 1 to October 15 (Monday through Saturday) and every day from October 15 through election day. To avoid problems associated with periodicity, we alternated sampling Monday, Wednesday, Friday (i.e., first week), and Tuesday, Thursday, and Saturday (i.e., second week). In addition, every Sunday was examined for the entire time period.

14. We did not restrict our analysis to campaign-related stories since citizens often acquire information about candidates in stories that are not directly related to the ongoing campaign (e.g., stories detailing a senator's work on legislation relevant to the state).

15. Intercoder reliability was assessed repeatedly during the coding process. On average, there was 92 percent agreement across the content codes. For more details about the newspaper content analysis methodology, see Kim Fridkin Kahn and Patrick J. Kenney, *The Spectacle of U.S. Senate Campaigns.*

16. In conducting the NES Senate Election Study, about sixty respondents in each state were randomly selected to be interviewed. The interviews were done by telephone and took place within two months of the 1988, 1990, and 1992 elections. In total, 9,253 interviews were completed, with 3,145 respondents interviewed in 1988, 3,349 individuals in 1990, and 2,759 respondents in 1992. The interviews averaged about thirty-five minutes in length. See Warren E. Miller, Donald R. Kinder, Steven J. Rosenstone, and the National Election Studies, *National Election Studies*, 1988, 1990, 1992, Pooled Senate Election Study (Ann Arbor, MI: University of Michigan, Center for Political Studies, 1999).

2

WHEN DO CANDIDATES GO NEGATIVE?

In the fall of 1998, just a few months after recovering from double-bypass surgery, Republican Senator Arlen Specter was campaigning to secure his fourth term in the U.S. Senate. He crisscrossed Pennsylvania, visiting all sixty-seven counties before election day. During one eighteen day stretch he canvassed thirty-five counties, conducting town meetings with potential voters. Across the state he emphasized his experience and how hard he had worked to improve the lives of his constituents. He stressed that after eighteen years in the Senate he knew how to help the people of Pennsylvania. Specter aired thirty-five radio spots in which constituents explained how Specter had solved or eased dramatic problems in their lives. He spent over $4.5 million on his campaign. Approximately 20 percent of his expenditures were aimed at producing and airing television commercials. He aired over five hundred spots in the television markets encompassing Philadelphia and Pittsburgh, and he sprinkled hundreds of other spots across the smaller markets in Pennsylvania, such as Wilkes-Barre and Harrisburg. First and foremost, Specter wanted people to know his record of accomplishment in the Senate. But Specter also wanted the voters of Pennsylvania to know that he would work diligently to protect Social Security, to increase funding for the National Institutes of Health, and to streamline government spending. Polls throughout the fall indicated that Specter was leading his opponent by as many as thirty points. The polls were accurate. On election day he beat his rival 61 percent to 35 percent. Specter would represent the people of Pennsylvania in the U.S. Senate into the new century, a job he started back in 1980.

Specter's opponent was former state representative William Lloyd. Lloyd spent only $187,157 campaigning against Specter. In 1998, in a state the size of Pennsylvania, this amount of money is tantamount to not campaigning at all. Lloyd aired no TV ads. He argued that he was an advocate for consumers. But, with no money, voters did not hear Lloyd's message. The major media outlets in Pennsylvania paid little attention to the race. Specter did agree to debate Lloyd, and, in one debate, Lloyd criticized Specter for voting against

Social Security. Shortly after the debate Specter's campaign produced a commercial that documented Specter's voting record on Social Security. This was the extent of negative campaigning in the Pennsylvania senate race that fall. In the last week of the campaign, Specter actually curtailed his advertising.

Campaigns have not always been so genteel for Specter. Six years earlier, in the "Year of the Women," Specter found himself in a donnybrook with Lynn Yeakel. A record-setting eleven women ran for the U.S. Senate in 1992. Yeakel was one of seven women challenging male incumbents. Yeakel decided to challenge Specter after she witnessed his "appalling" treatment of Anita Hill during the spectacle of Clarence Thomas's Senate confirmation hearings to the U.S. Supreme Court. Before the Senate Judiciary Committee, of which Specter was a member, Hill accused Thomas of sexual impropriety when they worked together at the Department of Education and then at the Equal Employment Opportunity Commission. Specter, along with several GOP senators on the committee, sided with Thomas and worked hard to discredit Hill's testimony before a nationwide TV audience in 1991. Thomas was eventually confirmed to the U.S. Supreme Court. Thomas's supporters considered Specter a champion, while Hill's supporters viewed Specter as a villain.

With the Thomas hearings as backdrop, it is not surprising that this race was competitive from the start. Polls throughout the fall showed the race "too close to call." Specter's lead never exceeded ten percentage points and was as low as two points in the last week of October. Specter spent over $10 million trying to hold his seat, and Yeakel spent over $5 million trying to take it away. As in 1998, Specter canvassed the state, campaigning in all sixty-seven counties, returning to some counties numerous times. He again stressed his record of accomplishment and his hard work for Pennsylvanians. He began his advertising campaign early, in late July. Yeakel stressed women's issues, such as child care, but she also focused on health care and the economy. Both candidates ran thousands of commercials on TV and radio.

In the end, though, this campaign was characterized by negativity on both sides. Specter and Yeakel attacked each other early and often, criticizing one another from September to election day, on TV, on radio, in the newspapers, and in debates. No topic was spared. Civility was set aside. The *Philadelphia Inquirer*, the largest circulating newspaper in the state, monitored the race from start to finish. The newspaper articles and headlines were replete with negativity. As an example, the paper reported extensively on an acrimonious debate on television. The candidates sparred about Specter's votes in the Senate, especially on the issues of education and Social Security. Exchanges between the candidates were testy. Yeakel dubbed Specter "Senator Flip-Flop," claiming he voted two different ways on an education bill on the same day. She claimed Specter "moved back and forth like the windshield wiper he is." Yeakel also claimed Specter was a latecomer to the problems of health care. Specter responded aggressively, "I've been working on that issue for 12 years." He pointed to his work on the Appropriations Committee as evidence of his attention to the issue of health care.

The candidates clashed on October 20 in a debate on the radio as well. Both candidates attacked one another. Specter made the sweeping claim that, "Yeakel was a single-issue candidate and she did not have command of the issues that one needs to be a member of the U.S. Senate." An article in the *Inquirer* the following day concluded, "Republican U.S. Senator Arlen Specter and Democratic challenger Lynn Yeakel pummeled each other yesterday in a radio debate that was characterized more by theatrics than substance. While each talked in generalities about solutions to the nation's ills, neither was shy with specifics about the other's flaws. Their interruptions of each other during the hour-long radio show, *Breakfast with the Candidates*, on KYW(1060) led moderators at one point to ask whether they believed voters really cared about all the personal attacks."

The negative campaign pressed beyond matters of national policy. Specter's campaign ran a commercial quoting news accounts that Yeakel paid more than $17,000 in back taxes the day before entering the Senate race. Yeakel responded with an ad of her own explaining that her failure to pay the taxes was inadvertent. Yeakel explained that she had paid almost 40 percent of her income to taxes and charitable contributions over the past five years. The tax controversy captured the attention of the candidates and the leading newspapers over several days in late September and early October.

The candidates' back and forth and to and fro continued across the entire campaign. The campaign reached a fever pitch during the last week. Four days before election day, Yeakel launched a new round of negative ads. Specter criticized Yeakel's commercials at nearly all campaign stops the last few days. Two days before election day, Yeakel campaigned with presidential candidate Bill Clinton. On election day, the candidates stumped tirelessly across the state. Yeakel campaigned eighteen hours nonstop by car, while Specter logged six hundred miles on the last day by air. In most speeches, at every stop, the candidates criticized one another. For example, Yeakel, at a plant packaging apples for shipping, encouraged supporters to "throw the bad apples out (of the Senate)." And, Specter, citing occasional gaffes by Yeakel over the preceding months, stressed that she "lacked the competence to serve in the U.S. Senate." In the end, on election day, Specter won by three percentage points, but captured less than a majority of voters, winning 49 percent to 46 percent.

Senator Specter's sojourn across two elections in the 1990s illustrates the conditions that lead candidates to conduct negative campaigns. Three forces conspire to bring about large doses of negative messages: the competitive nature of the race, the status of the candidate (i.e., incumbents or challengers), and the proximity to election day.[1] Specter's 1998 campaign was never competitive and the amount of negative discussion by the candidates was trivial. The 1992 campaign, competitive from start to finish, was negative from beginning to end.

TABLE 2.1　NEGATIVITY IN CANDIDATES' COMMERCIALS BY COMPETITION

	COMPETITIVE RACES			NONCOMPETITIVE RACES		
	POSITIVE ADS	NEGATIVE ADS		POSITIVE ADS	NEGATIVE ADS	
Incumbent	41%	59%	(50,758)	88%	12%	(15,592)
Challenger	43	56	(44,301)	46	54	(3,651)
Open Race Candidate	36	64	(8,544)	82	18	(7,789)

Source: Brennan Institute data from 1998 U.S. Senate Campaigns.

The Specter campaigns are not unique. In general, close races breed negative campaigns. In Table 2.1 we present the percent of negative advertisements generated by incumbents, challengers, and open seat candidates in the 1998 senatorial campaigns.[2] Tens of thousands of ads are examined here.[3] The pattern is clear. The percentage of negative ads increases as competition increases (see Table 2.1).[4] When polls indicate that the outcome of the race is uncertain, then candidates cannot simply tell voters why they should support their candidacies. Instead, the competitiveness of the race compels candidates to convince voters not to support their opponents. Politicians need to tell citizens why they should *not* vote for their opponents and this entails criticizing opponents across a wide range of topics, whenever money and time allows.

We also examine how competition influences candidates' reliance on negativity by relying on our panel survey of campaign managers.[5] Changes in competition from election to election are important for understanding changes in the same senator's reliance on negative campaigning. For example, six of the candidates in our sample experienced significantly less competitive campaigns in 1998, compared to 1992. While five of these six candidates (83 percent) engaged in negative campaigning in 1992, six years later, when their campaigns were less competitive, only one of the six (17 percent) relied on negative themes.

Furthermore, seven of the candidates in our sample faced noncompetitive races in 1992 *and* 1998. Only one of these candidates (14 percent) relied on negative themes in 1992 and none of these safe incumbents engaged in negative campaigning in 1998. Finally, six candidates faced competitive races in 1992 and 1998. And these candidates, as expected, relied heavily on negative themes in both years. In 1992, half of the candidates (50 percent) engaged in negative campaigning and in 1998, two-thirds of these vulnerable incumbents (67 percent) relied on negative themes.

Both cross-sectional data and over-time data show that the competitiveness of the race influences candidates' reliance on negativity. In addition to competition, the status of the candidate also alters when candidates go negative. Incumbents and challengers implement attack politics under different circumstances. In 1998, Lloyd attacked Specter sparingly, and Specter responded by producing only one political ad that countered Lloyd's charges. In 1992, Yeakel attacked Specter harshly throughout the race. Specter responded immediately and aggressively. Once again, Specter's races highlight a general pattern. An examination of all negative ads in the 1998 senate races demonstrate that challengers tend to criticize incumbents in all types of races, competitive or not (see Table 2.1). Fifty-six percent of challengers' ads are negative in competitive races and 54 percent are negative in noncompetitive races. Challengers need to provide reasons why voters should reject the incumbents—why the incumbents should be fired. Challengers, therefore, always need to produce negative messages about the incumbent.

However, like Lloyd, many challengers in noncompetitive races do not have the resources to disseminate criticisms of incumbents. In other words, many noncompetitive challengers do not have the money to air commercials. Lloyd was able to criticize Specter's voting record only during a debate. If Specter would not have agreed to a debate, then Lloyd's criticism would never have captured any publicity. In 1998, 46 percent of challengers in noncompetitive races were unable to produce commercials. In contrast, virtually all challengers (90 percent) in competitive races aired commercials.

Incumbents, on the other hand, are rarely at a loss for resources.[6] They fight back with negative attacks if they feel threatened by an uncertain outcome. In 1998, 59 percent of incumbents' commercials were negative in close races, while only 12 percent of incumbents' ads were negative in noncompetitive races. In 1998, in the nation's top media markets, incumbents in competitive races aired close to 51,000 negative ads. In contrast, incumbents facing noncompetitive races disseminated only 15,000 negative ads. Thus, incumbents generate over three times as many negative ads when they feel threatened by challengers, compared to incumbents who appear to be easy winners.

Finally, candidates competing in negative campaigns increase their attacks toward the end of the campaign. In 1998, Specter actually curtailed his advertising campaign in the final weeks of the election. In contrast, in 1992 Specter and Yeakel campaigned tirelessly the final week, blitzing each other in stump speeches and in television commercials. Again, Specter's races are representative of other senate campaigns. We examine the percent of negative ads produced by all senatorial candidates by week in 1998 (see Figure 2.1 on page 24). Ten weeks prior to Election Day in 1998, the candidates aired less than one percent of their negative spots on TV. Candidates gradually increased their negative ads until they reached a climax during the final week of the campaign. One-fourth of all negative ads appeared during the final seven days prior to election day. And approximately 60 percent of all negative ads are shown on TV during the final three weeks of the campaigns (25 percent + 18 percent + 17 percent). Candidates want voters to have at their fingertips multiple reasons to vote against their opponents as voters enter the ballot box. Candidates provide these reasons as close to election day as possible.

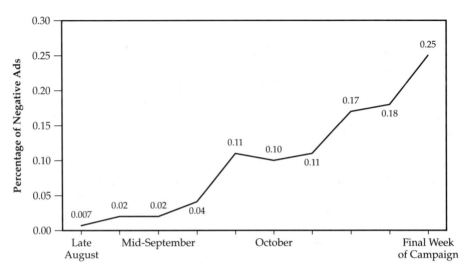

FIGURE 2.1   PERCENTAGE OF NEGATIVE ADS OVER TIME

Source: Brennan Institute data from the 1998 U.S. Senate Campaigns.

In summary, challengers tend to criticize incumbents. However, the ability and intensity of challengers' criticisms heighten dramatically if challengers feel they can win the race. Likewise, if the outcome of the race is uncertain, incumbents fight back fiercely. And, if polls show the race to be close in late October, challengers and incumbents attack one another viciously in the last few weeks of the campaign. But what is the content of these negative messages? It is clear that candidates know when to attack, but what do they say?

DESCRIBING THE CONTENT OF NEGATIVE MESSAGES

Once candidates decide to attack their opponents in U.S. Senate races, campaign managers, media strategists, advertising consultants, and pollsters spend large amounts of time and energy deciding the content of the attacks. Although candidates focus their negative messages on the general topics of issues and personal traits, they are far more likely to criticize their opponents on issues than on traits.[7] In the U.S. Senate races in 1998, 69 percent of the candidates' attack advertisements focused on issues, while 23 percent discussed personal traits, and 8 percent of the ads combined issue and trait discussion. The same pattern can be seen in contrast ads. In 1998, 74 percent of contrast ads examined the candidates on issues, while 16 percent made comparisons about traits, and 10 percent drew distinctions on issues and traits.[8]

When candidates criticize their opponents on issues, they tend to employ three strategies: They criticize the opponent's policy agenda; they attack the opponent's positions on specific issues; and they blame negative policy outcomes on the opponent.[9] Specter and Yeakel utilized all three strategies as they battered one another.

When candidates utilize the first strategy—criticizing the opponent's policy agenda—candidates want voters to know that their opponents intend to lead the nation astray on a series of issues. With this strategy, candidates critique the general policy direction that their opponents are extolling. In Pennsylvania, Yeakel attacked the specifics of Specter's policy agenda, whereas Specter attacked Yeakel for not having an agenda at all. Yeakel consistently linked Specter to the "Reagan-Bush-Quayle policies of allowing America's cities to crumble." She argued that since Reagan came to office in 1980, residents of Pennsylvania's cities struggled with finding quality housing, meaningful jobs, and affordable health care. Specter, in turn, contended that Yeakel never articulated an overall agenda. Instead, throughout the campaign, he asserted she was a "single-issue candidate" focusing all her attention on Specter's treatment of Anita Hill during the Clarence Thomas hearings before the Senate a year earlier. Specter, reacting to another Yeakel commercial discussing the Anita Hill affair, noted in the *Inquirer* on November 1, "She's back to a single issue, that's all she has. There is a lot more to representing Pennsylvania than a single issue."

In the second strategy, candidates hone in on an opponent's position on a specific issue. To locate specific policy positions, candidates often rely on the voting record of politicians and on policy statements made during campaign speeches or commercials. Yeakel criticized Specter for his votes on presidential appointments to federal courts, claiming that the Reagan-Bush appointees were too often white male appointments. Yeakel's statement on September 10 summed up her position, "It is staggering to think my opponent, who calls himself a moderate, voted to confirm all but four of 557 Reagan-Bush judicial nominees who have made all the federal courts the most conservative and anti-minority court in history. The federal judiciary should not be a bastion of rich, white men." Specter more than once criticized Yeakel's issue positions. For instance, Specter attacked Yeakel on Social Security for proposing a "cost-of-living-adjustment freeze" for senior citizens. He repeated throughout the campaign that Yeakel was "out-of-touch" with the issues facing citizens who have passed sixty-five years of age.

The final strategy is to explicitly link an opponent's issue positions to a general failure of government policy. The idea is to blame the opponent for broad policy failures. If at all possible, candidates would like voters to believe that opponents' positions actually contributed to large-scale policy failures. This strategy is used most frequently by challengers. Incumbent senators can be linked to policy problems by the simple virtue of being in office when bad things happen. In contrast, incumbents cannot easily tie challengers to policy disasters because they were not in office when problems arose. Yeakel took aim at the struggling economy in the early 1990s and explicitly linked Specter to the lackluster economic growth experienced during President George Bush's years in office. Yeakel, in a radio debate on October 3, claimed, "The recession was caused by 12 years of Republican administrations. He (Specter) has been part of the policies that the Reagan, Bush, Quayle administration have put forward."

While attacking the personal traits of opponents is not as popular as attacking issues, candidates do occasionally criticize their opponent's personality. Candidates commonly focus on leadership, integrity, background, and competence.[10] Challengers and incumbents, however, focus on different traits. Challengers like to focus on the incumbents' ties to the Washington establishment. The goal here is to imply that incumbents are taking advantage of perks that are only available to powerful U.S. senators. Campaigning in Pittsburgh on October 21, Yeakel criticized Specter for accepting a pay raise and using the congressional perk of free mail. In her own words, "It's a classic case of the arrogance of the people in Washington who keep getting more and more money. Arlen Specter has doubled his salary (over the previous 10 years). When he says he is fighting for our jobs, it sounds like he's fighting for his job." She was not done quite yet. On the same campaign swing, she asserted, "The recession hasn't reached Capitol Hill, Arlen Specter sent out $1 million worth of taxpayer-paid mailings last year by using his congressional franking privilege."

Incumbents, on the other hand, tend to talk about their opponents lack of experience. Yeakel, of course, had never held public office. She had no official connections in the Congress. In addition, in 1992, Pennsylvania's other senator was Harris Wofford who had been elected in a special election in 1991. In his messages Specter highlighted that Yeakel would be a senatorial neophyte while Senator Wofford was a mere freshman. He repeated the phrase frequently across the state, "It won't do for Pennsylvania to be represented by two junior senators." He emphasized his experience at drafting legislation (e.g., he stressed that he coauthored legislation to obtain money for the homeless in 1983—$50 million) and he emphasized his power on the appropriations subcommittee (e.g., he explained that he took the lead to find funding for Healthy Start). He asserted that Pennsylvanians would reap the benefits of having an "insider" in the Senate as opposed to yet another "outsider" representing the citizens of Pennsylvania.

THE DYNAMIC NATURE OF NEGATIVE MESSAGES BY POLITICAL PARTIES

The Democratic and Republican parties developed a new role in campaigns during the 1990s. Both parties, mostly via soft money, began producing and airing negative political advertisements. In fact, since 1996 there had been a revolution in the rise of noncandidate advertisements. In the 2000 senatorial campaigns, political parties spent almost $40 million producing ads, while interest groups spent over $10 million creating their own set of commercials. Advertising by parties and interest groups accounted for almost 30 percent of all messages in the 2000 senate races (i.e., 22 percent by parties and 6 percent by interest groups).[11]

Most of the advertising by these groups is classified as "issue advocacy advertising." Parties and interest groups faced few federal restrictions when they relied on issue advocacy advertising. For example, if groups did not *explicitly* advocate support for a candidate (i.e., use the "magic" words such as "vote for Candidate X" or "support candidate Y"), then they could spend as much as they wanted producing or airing commercials during electoral campaigns. According to a recent report by the Brennan Institute, political parties became quite ingenious at supporting a candidate without explicitly using the "magic" words. In fact, in the 2000 election cycle, more than 90 percent of all party ads were candidate advocacy ads.[12] While these advertisements did not use the "magic words," the commercials were clearly aimed at either increasing support for a particular candidate or decreasing support for the opposing candidate. Interest groups are less likely to air advocacy ads for candidates. Only 30 percent of the advertisements by interest groups advocated support for a particular candidate in 2000, while almost 70 percent of the ads provided information about issues.

In the last two election cycles, political parties spent almost four times as much money as interest groups did on advertising. Relying on the Brennan Institute for data on advertising in the 1998 senate elections, we examine the amount and content of party advertisements (see Figure 2.2 on page 28).[13] In general, parties were strategic with their ads. They spent money in races with uncertain outcomes, and in these races they were likely to attack their party's opponent. Overall, party advertising was much more negative than candidate advertising. In particular, party commercials in competitive races were uniformly negative, irrespective of the status of the candidate. Parties were equally likely to attack incumbents, challengers, and candidates in open races. The only races in which the messages disseminated by parties were positive were in noncompetitive races; this is especially true for challengers. Of course, parties ran few commercials in these lopsided races.

In Specter's 1998 race, in which he strolled to easy victory, the Republican Party did not produce ads supporting Specter, and the Democratic Party saw no reason to spend money on ads trying to elect Lloyd. But while Specter was relaxing, just across the Pennsylvania state line to the north, New York incumbent Senator Alfonse D'Amato was struggling to hold his seat. He too was a Republican and he had come to the Senate with Specter in 1980. In 1992 when Specter had his hands full with Yeakel, D'Amato almost lost to Democrat Robert Abrams, winning by only 1 percentage point. He and Specter both captured 49 percent of the vote in 1992.

In 1998 D'Amato found himself in yet another race in which the outcome was uncertain. D'Amato's opponent was Democratic Congressmen Charles

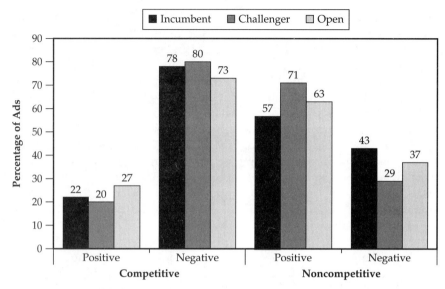

FIGURE 2.2 THE TONE OF PARTY ADS BY COMPETITION

Source: Brennan Institute data from the 1998 U.S. Senate Campaigns.

Schumer. Schumer was an eighteen-year veteran of the House of Representatives. He was energetic, he was adept at raising money, and he loved to campaign. In short order, this race became intensely negative. The candidates moved quickly to attack one another, at times viciously. There was playground style name-calling. For example, in front of the press, or in ads, D'Amato and Schumer called one another "liar," "hypocrite," "devoid of integrity," "a pit-bull dog," and on one occasion, although somewhat disputed, D'Amato described Schumer with an ethnic slur. Beyond the personal attacks, the candidates criticized the content of their respective campaign messages as "useless," "bankrupt of ideas," "fraudulent," "mind-numbing," "irrelevant," and "desperate."

Holding aside the vicious nature of the campaign between the two combatants, D'Amato was also being bombarded by ads produced and aired by the Democratic Party—a lot of ads. The Democratic Party spent $3.2 million on ads aimed at defeating D'Amato. The Democrats were relentless. In the top five media markets in New York state (New York City, Buffalo, Rochester, Albany, and Syracuse), the Democratic Party aired 3,831 ads. In 66 percent of the ads, the messages were entirely negative. Schumer ran another 13,784 ads in the same media markets, spending $14.8 million. Schumer spent a total of $16 million in his challenge to D'Amato. In contrast to the party's ads, however, only 26 percent of Schumer's ads were exclusively negative. Between the Democratic Party and Schumer, 6,111 negative ads were run against D'Amato in the top five media markets.

D'Amato and the Republicans were not to be outdone. If D'Amato lost, the Democrats would have two senators from New York; popular Democratic Senator Patrick Moynihan held the other seat. D'Amato spent $24 million on the race; $14 million went to advertising. He aired 17,294 commercials in the top five media markets; 42 percent were exclusively negative. The Republican Party supplied an additional 4,313 ads aimed at Schumer, which cost the Republican Party $2.2 million. Sixty-four percent of these ads were entirely negative. D'Amato and the Republicans hurled 10,023 exclusively negative ads at Schumer, almost doubling the ads Shumer and the Democrats aimed at D'Amato. In terms of party advertising and specifically negative party advertising in 1998, the political parties fought the hardest in New York. Although the parties worked tirelessly in other states in 1998 (e.g., North Carolina), none of the party efforts surpassed New York. This was a race that neither party wanted to lose and both parties thought they could win.

In the end, after all the commercials, after all the negative critiques, D'Amato lost by nearly 10 percentage points. Between D'Amato's narrow victory in 1992 and his devastating loss in 1998, the politics and strategies of negative advertising had changed. In 1992, he battled plenty of negative ads, thousands in fact, but virtually all were paid for and produced by Abrams. In 1998, Schumer had plenty of help from the Democratic Party when it came to attacking D'Amato.

The new party strategies that began in 1996 and were in full bloom in 1998 and 2000 were suddenly thwarted in the spring of 2002. In March 2002, the Congress passed and President George W. Bush signed legislation radically altering the campaign finance system for federal elections for the first time since the 1970s. The legislation had direct implications for the parties' use of negative issue advocacy advertisements. Specifically, soft money, the primary fuel for issue advocacy ads, was banned altogether, and issue advocacy ads were prohibited from airing within sixty days of the general election. The vast majority of the parties' issue advocacy ads from 1996 to 2002 hit the airwaves in the final weeks of the fall campaign—this will no longer be the case. The legislation took affect immediately following the 2000 election. So in 2004, the parties will have to fundamentally alter their strategies.

RELIANCE ON NEGATIVE CAMPAIGNING BY MALE AND FEMALE CANDIDATES

Thus far, we have shown that negative campaigning is conditioned by a host of forces, including the closeness of the race, the status of the candidates, and proximity to election day. However, an additional factor needs to be considered: the gender of the candidate. In the 1992 Pennsylvania senate race, both Arlen Specter and Lynn Yeakel engaged in a great deal of negative campaigning. But was this race typical? Are women as likely as men to rely on negative messages? If so, do women rely on different types of negative advertising, compared to their male counterparts? Are men reluctant to use negative advertisements when running against women?

Explaining gender differences in the use of negative appeals is important given the growing number of women running for the U.S. Senate.[14] Over the last six elections (i.e., 1990, 1992, 1994, 1996, 1998, 2000), fifty-three women have run for the U.S. Senate as major party candidates. This is nearly twice the number of women who competed for the U.S. Senate in the previous six elections. Between 1978 and 1988 (i.e., 1978, 1980, 1982, 1984, 1986, 1988), only twenty-eight women ran for the U.S. Senate. In addition, women are more likely to run as incumbents today, compared to the past. In the 107th Congress (2001–2003), thirteen women serve as U.S. senators. Ten years ago, in the 101st Congress (1989–1991), there were only two female senators.

To examine whether men and women use negative appeals differently, we look at negative advertisements by candidates running for the U.S. Senate during the 1988, 1990, and 1992 elections. During this period, twenty-one women ran for election to the U.S. Senate; nineteen of these candidates were nonincumbents.

One of the first decisions facing male and female candidates is whether their ads should be exclusively negative or comparative in content. That is, should the commercial be focused entirely on the weaknesses of the opponent? Or should the ad contain some information that compares the candidate with the opponent? Both types of commercials contain negative information about the opponent. However, the attack advertisement provides no information about the candidate airing the attack; while the comparative advertisement contrasts the candidate airing the advertisement with the opponent. We intend to examine whether men and women differ in their use of attack and comparative ads.

Once candidates decide to produce attack or comparative ads, they then choose specific topics to emphasize in their ads. In particular, the candidates decide if the advertisement will focus on policy matters or the personal characteristics of the candidates. Do men and women differ when it comes to attacking their opponents' issue priorities and positions? And, do men and women differ in their likelihood of criticizing their opponents' personal traits? In Hillary Clinton's 2000 campaign against Rick Lazio, Clinton often relied on negative issue commercials to paint an unfavorable portrait of her opponent. Clinton ran one advertisement, for example, where an announcer intones

> The End to Nursing Home Standards. The Largest Education Cuts in History. The Slashing of Medicare by $270 billion dollars. Who voted for all this? Rick Lazio. With Rick Lazio, the more you know . . . the more you wonder.

Two years earlier in New York, Chuck Shumer used many negative trait commercials in his successful 1988 campaign against Senator Alfonso D'Amato. During the campaign, Schumer attacked D'Amato's character in a series of negative commercials with the tag line, "Al D'Amato is still lying. D'Amato—too many lies for too long."

Finally, irrespective of the content of negative commercials, candidates differ in the number of criticisms presented in their negative commercials. We can compare the number of criticisms in the advertisements aired by male and female candidates in the 1988–1992 senate campaigns. It may be the case that men and women air the same number of negative advertisements; however, the commercials generated by male and female candidates may differ in the raw number of criticisms contained in the advertisements.

We begin by looking at incumbents and nonincumbents separately since our earlier analysis shows that negative campaigning is more common for nonincumbents.[15] Turning first to incumbents, we find that the two female senators in our sample (Senator Nancy Kassebaum of Kansas and Senator Barbara Mikulski of Maryland) never aired negative commercials in their reelection campaigns. Although the small number of female senators does not allow for informative comparisons with male incumbents, it is noteworthy that male senators relied on negative themes in about one-quarter of their advertisements.[16]

Turning to nonincumbents, where the number of female candidates is much greater, we examine five comparisons of negative messages by men and women (see Figure 2.3 on page 32). The first two columns on the left present the percentage of attack and comparative ads by men and women. The next two columns compare the use of negative messages in trait and issue ads by men and women. And the last column on the far right presents the raw number of criticisms in commercials by male and female candidates.

Women who are nonincumbents consistently use negative appeals less often than their male counterparts (see Figure 2.3 on page 32). On each of the five comparisons of negativity, women are less likely than male candidates to air negative messages. The differences are most sharp in the production of negative ads focusing on issues. For example, 40 percent of the commercials aired by male nonincumbents criticize their opponents concerning issues. Female nonincumbents, however, use negative issue advertisements only 30 percent of the time.

We continue our examination of gender differences in negative appeals by comparing men and women running in competitive and noncompetitive races (see Figure 2.4 on page 33). Men respond more dramatically to changes in the competitiveness of their races. In close races, male candidates are far more likely to employ all types of negative messages compared to noncompetitive races, with the exception of comparative ads. The sharpest change for men is evident in the use of negative issue ads. In competitive races, 42 percent of negative ads focus on issues. In contrast, in noncompetitive races, only 26 percent of the male candidates' negative ads examine issues.

Women, in contrast, react less powerfully and less consistently to the competitiveness of the race. For example, the reliance on attack ads for female

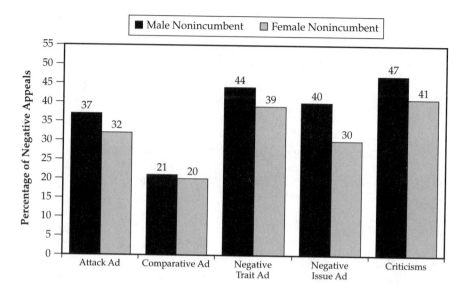

FIGURE 2.3   GENDER DIFFERENCES IN NEGATIVE APPEALS BY NONINCUMBENTS

Source: Kahn and Kenney's content analysis of political advertisements (1988–1992).

candidates is identical in competitive and noncompetitive races (30 percent). For other measures, negativity actually increases in noncompetitive races (e.g., negative trait ads). Overall, the use of negative messages by women does not differ markedly in close and lopsided races.

Two campaigns from 1998 illustrate the general differences between men and women in their use of negative messages. Both campaigns were in the Midwest, one in Illinois and one in Ohio. In Illinois, the incumbent was a woman, Democrat Carol Moseley-Braun, and the challenger was Republican Peter Fitzgerald. In Ohio, Republican George Voinovich and Democrat Mary Boyle were competing for an open seat. In mid-October, both men were leading in the polls. Peter Fitzgerald in Illinois was ahead by only ten points and polls in Ohio had George Voinovich leading by as many as twenty points.

The men in these two contests differed in their use of negative appeals, most likely reacting to the closeness of their campaigns. In Illinois, approximately 40 percent of Peter Fitzgerald's ads were exclusively negative. On Chicago TV stations, watched by two-thirds of the state's voters, nearly 1,300 negative ads blitzed the airwaves; and the Republican Party aired an additional 545 ads spots, all negative. In contrast, only 5 percent of Carol Moseley-Braun's commercials were exclusively negative. In the Chicago media market, she aired about 34 negative spots. The Democratic Party tried to help. The Democratic Party hit Peter Fitzgerald with nearly 100 negative ads in the greater Chicago area.

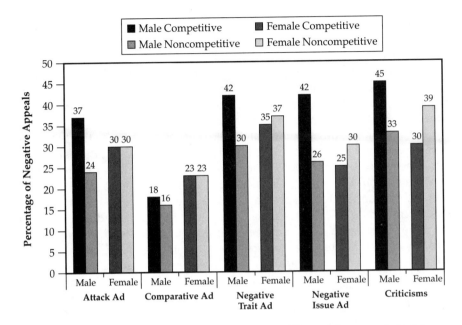

FIGURE 2.4   HOW COMPETITION INFLUENCES THE USE OF NEGATIVE APPEALS

Source: Kahn and Kenney's content analysis of political advertisements (1988–1992).

In metropolitan Chicago, then, Peter Fitzgerald and associates aired over 1,800 exclusively negative ads aimed at Carol Mosley-Braun, and she answered, with the help of the Democratic Party, with less than 150 exclusively negative ads. No doubt some of the discrepancy between the candidates was due to Peter Fitzgerald's ability to spend nearly $3.6 million more than Carol Moseley-Braun on advertising. Still, Carol Moseley-Braun spent over $1.7 million on advertising; she simply decided not to attack. In the end, Peter Fitzgerald won. But in the last week of October, Peter Fitzgerald's lead evaporated and he hung on to win by only three percentage points, 50 percent to 47 percent.

In Ohio, George Voinovich stayed securely ahead in the polls throughout the campaign. Voinovich won by twelve percentage points, defeating Mary Boyle 56 percent to 44 percent. George Voinovich aired 4,511 ads in the top five media markets in Ohio (i.e., Cleveland, Columbus, Cincinnati, Dayton, Toledo). Five percent of these ads were exclusively negative. The rest of his ads, a whopping 95 percent, were promotional ads that never mentioned Mary Boyle's name. Mary Boyle ran 1,098 ads in the same markets; none were exclusively negative. The Democratic Party, however, went negative, aiming 270 exclusively negative ads at George Voinovich in the top five markets. In contrast, the Republican Party aired no exclusively negative ads criticizing Mary Boyle.

So, Carol Mosley-Braun and Mary Boyle, like most female candidates, were less negative than their male opponents, irrespective of competition. And, true to the general patterns in the data presented earlier, Peter Fitzgerald and George Voinovich reacted strongly to competition. Peter Fitzgerald, battling an incumbent, pressed hard to criticize Carol Mosley-Braun. George Voinovich, on the other hand, with leads as high as twenty points and never below fifteen points, barely went negative.

Beyond illustrating the general patterns we observed with the 1988–1992 data, these two examples beg one remaining question about the use of negative messages by men and women: Do male candidates modify their reliance on negativity when campaigning against a female candidate? Given established gender stereotypes, male candidates may be hesitant to attack a female candidate because the public may view the male candidate as "beating up on the woman."[17] Does this explain why George Voinovich and the Republican Party limited their attacks on Mary Boyle? But in Illinois, Peter Fitzgerald consistently attacked Carol Moseley-Braun. Was it because the race was closer in Illinois than in Ohio? To answer these questions we contrast the use of negative messages by male candidates when they are battling male versus female opponents.

For this final analysis, we examine two measures of negative campaigning: (1) the use of negative ads; and (2) the percentage of ads containing criticisms of the male candidates' opponent.[18] In addition, because we discovered that men are more likely to go negative in competitive races, we look at their behavior in competitive and noncompetitive races.

Overall, in competitive races, men produce negative advertisements over half of the time (56 percent) when facing a male opponent and slightly over one-third of the time (39 percent) when facing a female opponent (see Figure 2.5). A similar finding is evident in the use of criticisms. In competitive races, men criticize other men in 48 percent of their ads, but they criticize female candidates in only 26 percent of their ads. In noncompetitive races, men are still more likely to run negative ads against male opponents and they are more likely to criticize male opponents than female opponents. However, the overall amount of negative commercials declines sharply when competition eases.

Male candidates, while significantly less likely to criticize a female opponent than a male opponent, do not completely refrain from using negative appeals. For example, in the 2000 New York race between Rick Lazio and Hillary Clinton, Lazio often criticized Clinton in his ads. In one Lazio commercial, Lazio uses Clinton's negative campaigning as a way to launch his own attacks. In this advertisement, an announcer explains that "Hillary Clinton is on the attack. The *Daily News* says her ads 'twist the truth to the breaking point.' The fact is while Mrs. Clinton was selling the Lincoln Bedroom to campaign donors, Rick Lazio was standing up to the Republican leadership and voting for McCain-Feingold."

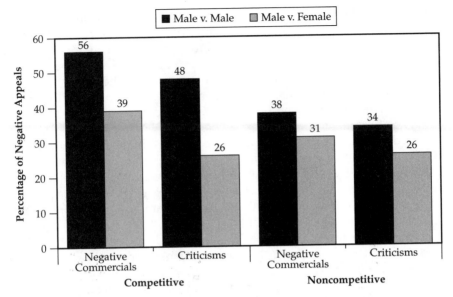

FIGURE 2.5   HOW THE GENDER OF THE OPPONENT AFFECTS MALE CANDIDATES' USE OF NEGATIVE APPEALS

Source: Kahn and Kenney's content analysis of political advertisements (1988–1992).

While Lazio did not refrain from attacking his female opponent, male candidates, in general, are more reluctant to criticize their female opponents than their male rivals.[19] In addition, our findings show that men and women differ in their reliance on negative appeals. In particular, we find that men are more likely to engage in negative campaigning, when compared to their female colleagues.

SUMMARY

What have we learned? Candidates do not employ negative messages randomly. They are strategic, using negative campaign themes only under certain circumstances. First, candidates go negative when the outcome of the race is uncertain. If polls indicate the race is competitive, then candidates use negative messages in order to build a case against their opponents (e.g., Specter vs. Yeakel, 1992). They critique their opponents in order to identify tangible reasons for citizens to vote against their opponent. More often than not, these reasons center squarely on the opponents' issue agendas and issue positions.

Second, challengers, all things being equal, are more likely to use negative messages than are incumbents (e.g., Yeakel, 1992; Fitzgerald, 1998). Citizens are unlikely to abandon the senator who has represented them for the last six years, at least, not without cause. Challengers need to make a case for why voters should change course and support someone new. They tend to rely on criticisms that blame incumbents for failed policies. They also try to explain to citizens that the incumbents have been corrupted by their ties to the "Washington Establishment."

Third, if incumbents appear to have a safe lead in the polls, they tend to avoid using negative messages altogether (e.g., Specter, 1998). They have no incentive to mention the challengers by name when they are well ahead in the polls. However, when incumbents feel challenged, they readily engage in negative campaigning and devote a significant amount of resources to attacking challengers (e.g., Specter, 1992; D'Amato, 1998).

Fourth, as election day approaches, negative themes are more prevalent. Candidates criticize their opponents more frequently and more harshly the last three weeks of the campaign, from mid-October to election day. Candidates want voters to have reasons to vote against the opponents on hand as they enter the voting booth.

Fifth, men make use of negative messages more often than women do. Irrespective of the status of the candidate or the closeness of the race, men are more likely to criticize their opponents than are women. Interestingly enough, men are also more critical of other male opponents than female opponents. These gender differences undoubtedly reflect societal norms concerning what is acceptable behavior for men and women in the public arena.

With a clear sense about when candidates go negative, it is time to turn to an investigation of how the press covers negative campaigns. Most senators have millions of constituents who are busy with their daily lives and seldom pay close attention to campaigns. The vast majority of citizens do not attend campaign rallies, or make appointments to visit U.S. senators, or watch candidates' commercials on TV. It is easy to flip TV stations or to mute political commercials on the TV or radio. After all, most citizens are fully aware that candidates' ads are campaign propaganda and must be viewed with skepticism.

In contrast, the press is ubiquitous. Newspapers, magazines, radio, and TV constantly invade citizens' lives at work, in the car, and at home. In addition, citizens are more likely to trust the information coming through the news media than information emanating from the candidates' campaigns.

Also, citizens who are most likely to vote are likely to be avid consumers of the contemporary press. Compared to nonvoters, they are much more likely to read a paper, follow the news on the radio while commuting to work, and watch the evening news on television. We need to know how the news media deals with the negative information that candidates disseminate during campaigns. We turn to this topic in the next chapter.

NOTES

1. Kim Fridkin Kahn and Patrick J. Kenney, *The Spectacle of U.S. Senate Campaigns* (Princeton, NJ: Princeton University Press, 1999); Paul S. Herrnson, *Congressional Elections: Campaigning at Home and in Washington* (Washington, D.C.: Congressional Quarterly Press, 1995); Mark C. Westlye, *Senate Elections and Campaign Intensity* (Baltimore, MD: Johns Hopkins University Press, 1991).
2. A negative commercial was any commercial containing criticisms of the opponent. Both attack ads (e.g., ads focusing exclusively on the opponent) and comparative ads (e.g., ads comparing the candidate with the opponent) are considered negative ads in this analysis.
3. This advertising data comes from the Brennan Institute. See Jonathan S. Krasno and Daniel E. Seltz, *Buying Time: Television Advertising in the 1998 Congressional Elections* (New York: Brennan Center for Justice at New York University School of Law or <buyingtime.org>, 2000).
4. We considered any race in which polls indicated that the candidates were separated by ten points or less as competitive.
5. See Chapter 1 for more information about this panel survey.
6. See Benjamin A. Webster, Clyde Wilcox, Paul S. Herrnson, Peter L. Fancia, John C. Green, and Lynda Powell, "Competing for Cash: The Individual Financiers of Congressional Elections," in *Playing Hardball: Campaigning for the U.S. Congress*, ed. Paul S. Herrnson (Upper Saddle River, NJ: Prentice Hall, 2001).
7. Kim Fridkin Kahn and Patrick J. Kenney, *The Spectacle of U.S. Senate Campaigns*; Paul S. Herrnson, *Congressional Elections: Campaigning at Home and in Washington*; Edie N. Goldenberg and Michael W. Traugott, *Campaigning for Congress* (Washington, D.C.: Congressional Quarterly Press, 1984).
8. As before, the 1998 data are from the Brennan Institute.
9. Our data from 1988 to 1992 reveal that these strategies are used about equally.
10. See Kim Fridkin Kahn and Patrick J. Kenney, *The Spectacle of U.S. Senate Campaigns*.
11. This information comes from <www.brennancenter.org>.
12. For information on this data, see Jonathan S. Krasno and Daniel E. Seltz, *Buying Time: Television Advertising in the 1998 Congressional Elections* (New York: Brennan Center for Justice at New York University School of Law or <buyingtime.org>, 2000).
13. See Krasno and Seltz, *Buying Time: Television Advertising in the 1998 Congressional Elections*.
14. There is a burgeoning literature examining when and why female candidates campaign differently than their male counterparts. See, for example, Susan J. Carroll, *Women as Candidates in American Politics* (Bloomington, IN: Indiana University Press, 1985); Richard Logan Fox, *Gender Dynamics in Congressional Elections* (Thousand Oaks, CA: Sage Publications, 1997); Kim F. Kahn, *The Political Consequences of Being a Woman: How Stereotypes Influence the Content and Impact of Statewide Campaigns* (New York: Columbia University Press, 1996).
15. We combine open candidates and challengers in this analysis because of the small number of female candidates.
16. Senator Kassebaum and Senator Mikulski were both running in noncompetitive races and we know negativity is less common in these low-key races.
17. Leonie Huddy and Nayda Terkildsen, "Gender Stereotypes and the Perception of Male and Female Candidates," *American Journal of Political Science* 37 (1993): 119–147; Kim F. Kahn, *The Political Consequences of Being a Woman*; Karen S. Johnson-Cartee and Gary A. Copeland, *Inside Political Campaigns: Theory and Practice* (Westport, CT: Praeger, 1997).
18. We combine attack advertisements and comparative advertisements here. The results remain the same if we distinguish between attack advertisements and comparative advertisements.
19. Kahn (Kim F. Kahn, *The Political Consequences of Being a Woman*) finds a similar pattern looking at an earlier period (1982–1986).

3

WHEN DOES THE PRESS GO NEGATIVE?

In Nebraska, governors and former governors often become U.S. senators. The most recent example is Ben Nelson. Nelson, a Democrat, ran for the U.S. Senate in 1996 while serving as the governor of Nebraska. Nelson lost his bid to an unknown candidate, Chuck Hagel.[1] Even though Nelson finished his term as governor, he did not seek reelection to the statehouse in 1998. Instead, in 2000, now former governor Ben Nelson launched a second campaign for the U.S. Senate. He won. He defeated Don Stenberg in the closest senatorial election in Nebraska since the state's first popular election of senators in 1916.

The story of Ben Nelson's rise and fall and rise again captured the attention of Nebraska's politicos and press corps for the better part of five years. To be sure, in Nebraska, political campaigns coincide with the fall campaigns of the Nebraska Cornhuskers. And, although the saga of "Big Red" football dominates the sports pages, Nelson's sojourn to the U.S. Senate was front-page news.

The largest circulating paper in the state, the Omaha *World-Herald*, diligently followed Nelson's ups and downs. Since 1889, the citizens of Omaha and surrounding communities have been receiving the news of the day from the *World Herald*. Politicians pay close attention to stories that appear in the paper because it is seen by a sizable proportion of the state's voting population. Omaha is the largest city in Nebraska, with nearly one-quarter of the population of Nebraska living in and around Omaha. Candidates seeking a seat in the U.S. Senate from Nebraska must campaign long and hard in Omaha. And, maybe most importantly, they must capture the attention of the editors and reporters at the *World-Herald*.

The stories printed in the *World-Herald* about Nelson's two attempts to win a U.S. Senate seat were quite different in 1996 than in 2000, especially in terms of negativity. In particular, negative coverage dominated campaign coverage in 2000, while press attention was significantly less negative in 1996. In this chapter we explain the variation in the tone of press coverage in senate campaigns by exploring the factors that produce negative news attention. In the Nebraska case, the readers of the *World-Herald* were flooded with nearly three times more articles focusing on negative campaign messages in 2000 than in 1996. From October 1 to election day in 1996, 13 percent of the headlines dealing with campaign stories about Nelson included a negative message. In contrast, from October 1 to election day in 2000, 37 percent of the headlines focusing on stories about Nelson displayed a negative message.

Beyond the headlines, the stories in 2000 focused on negative messages in much more detail than in 1996. In 2000, reporters and editors spent a great deal of time and space examining the candidates' ads, with special attention to the negative ads. Specifically, the *World-Herald* often reported the exact content of the candidates' negative ads and aggressively checked the accuracy of the charges in the ads. For example, on October 15, 2000, the *World Herald* ran an article with the headline, "Misleading Ads Attack Stenberg." The article examined one of Nelson's ads criticizing Stenberg's position on safe drinking water. The article, nearly 1,200 words long, juxtaposed the content of Nelson's ad against Stenberg's prior statements point-by-point. There were numerous other instances where the paper examined closely the accuracy of the candidates' ads, as these headlines illustrate: "How Ad Claims Compare with Record"; or, "Truth Elusive in Senate Ads: TV Commercials for Stenberg and Nelson Play Liberally with the Facts to Suit the Candidates' Purposes"; or, "Stenberg Criticizes TV Ads: Republican Calls Commercials by Nelson Hypocritical, While Democrat Talks about his Record and Senate Plans."

In addition, for many negative ads, the newspaper investigated the group or party paying for the commercial. For example, on October 20, 2000, the *World-Herald* ran an article with the headline, "Ads Criticize Nelson Over Right to Work." Although the fundamental charge in the ad claimed Nelson opposed "right-to-work laws," the author spent most of the article discussing the fact that the commercial was paid for by the National Right to Work Committee. He noted that Nebraska was one of four senatorial races where the group was running ads against Democrats with links to organized labor unions. The author emphasized that the group intended to spend over $100,000 running ads in the Omaha and Lincoln TV markets.

Editors at the paper also decided to examine the candidates' issue positions and they outlined specific comparisons between the candidates. In addition, the *World-Herald* carefully documented charges by one candidate and allowed space for the opponent's rebuttal. And the paper did not shy away from reporting harsh exchanges between the candidates. Even if the charges were ad hominem in tone, the paper printed a great deal of what the candidates had to say. For example, a story with the headline "Senate Race Ads get Dirty as Election Nears," was filled with charges and counter-charges by the candidates. On election day, two authors summing up the campaign titled their article, "Stenberg, Nelson Spar to the End." They observed,

> Republican Don Stenberg and Ben Nelson each made a last dash here Monday, each with the goal of convincing Nebraskans to give him renewed political life at the ballot box today. The U.S. Senate contest between the longtime rivals began in Grand Island the day after the May 9 primary with a handshake. But with angry words exchanged even on the last day of the campaign, a final face-to-face meeting was avoided here as Nelson boarded his campaign airplane just as Stenberg's landed.

In contrast, in 1996, the *World-Herald* had far less to say about negativity. To be sure, both candidates were less negative in 1996 than in 2000. In 1996, both candidates pledged not to attack one another in ads or on the campaign trail. Nonetheless, and not unexpectedly, these promises were broken in late October with a short but rather nasty exchange between Nelson and Hagel. Nelson had led by as many as twenty points in the polls in September. But by mid-October, his lead had shrunk to approximately ten points. Both candidates went negative. Hagel's charges were direct and related directly to governing. He criticized Nelson for seeking a senatorial seat while he still had responsibilities as governor and Hagel also criticized Nelson for raising property taxes while governor. Nelson attacked Hagel both politically and personally. He charged that Hagel wanted to reduce student loans. But more dramatically, he questioned how Hagel put together a successful cellular telephone company, hinting that Hagel's practices were "in apparent violation of the law." Both candidates countered with ads challenging and refuting the other's charges.

Headlines in articles between mid-October and election day indicate that the *World-Herald* was interested in the candidates' exchanges: on October 19, 1996, "Hagel, Nelson Bringing Out Hard-Hitting TV Attack Ads"; on October 27, 1996, "Nelson Abandons the High Road as Nebraska Senate Race Tightens"; on October 30, 1996, "Hagel, Nelson Lash Out as Campaign Nears End." While the paper was tracking the candidates' attacks, editors and reporters did not invest the same amount of time and energy examining the content and accuracies of the candidates' charges compared to 2000. The most common similarity between the coverage of negative messages in 2000 and 1996 was that the *World-Herald* allowed the candidates to refute one another in the paper. Direct attacks were reported verbatim and replies were quoted directly.

Why did the *World-Herald* vary its coverage across the two elections? Typically, the differences in coverage would be the result of different candidates. But Ben Nelson was the key player in both races. Often, differences in coverage result from differences in the status of the candidates, that is, races with or without incumbent senators. Yet both races were open as retiring incumbents created a vacuum in Nebraska politics. Are the differences traceable to different reporters? No. Journalists C. David Kotok, Paul Goodsell, and David Hendee authored many articles together and separately in both campaigns. These reporters were making a living covering the adventures of Ben Nelson. Does the year of the election help explain the different treatments of negativity? In presidential election years, local candidates often receive less attention from the press as editors and reporters allocate considerable amounts of space to the presidential campaign.[2] Nelson pursued the U.S. Senate in presidential election years both times.

The most likely explanation rests with two key differences between the 1996 and 2000 campaigns: the behavior of the candidates, and the closeness of the races. In 2000, Nelson and Stenberg went negative from the beginning of the campaign and stayed negative to the end. In 1996, Nelson and Hagel did not attack one another until mid-to-late October. In 2000, there were months of negativity involving numerous negative ads and a great deal of back-and-forth by the candidates. In 1996, there were only a few weeks of this type of behavior. Reporters and editors wrote about negativity in 2000 because that is what the campaign was about. In 1996, in contrast, there was less negativity in print because there were fewer negative messages offered by the candidates.

Turning to competition as an explanation, although both races were close toward the end, in 1996 Nelson had led by as many as twenty points in late September of 1996. By mid-to-late October Nelson's lead had narrowed, and by early November his lead in the polls had evaporated entirely. A poll published by the *World-Herald* less than a week before election day indicated the race was "a dead-heat." Not surprisingly, negative attacks by the two candidates correlated perfectly with the changing poll numbers. The first round of negative ads appeared in mid-October, and by early November the negativity between Nelson and Hegal reached its peak. In 2000, Nelson had only a marginal lead in September; by early October Nelson's lead was gone completely and the race was "too close to call." Thus, the 2000 campaign was competitive for nearly ten weeks, while the 1996 race was close for only two to three weeks.

As the Nebraska campaigns show, the citizens of Omaha and surrounding communities had a great deal more negative information at their disposal in 2000 than they did in 1996. Although the unfolding story of Ben Nelson's pursuit of a seat in the U.S. Senate is illustrative, we need to investigate campaigns and newspapers beyond Nebraska. The content of the press's reporting of senatorial campaigns is an important aspect of the citizens' information environment. We are most interested in the negative messages in this environment. What does negative newspaper coverage look like? Why are there large amounts of negative coverage in some newspapers, while few criticisms turn up in other papers? We turn now to an examination of these questions.

Patterns of Negative Coverage

Distracted voters first come in contact with negative campaign messages via headlines. Headlines provide cues for the information contained in articles, but they also communicate messages directly to readers. In many instances, readers can glean negative messages by simply reading the headline. For example, headlines in the *World-Herald* in the last week of the 2000 Nelson-Stenberg race painted a clear picture that these two candidates had been battling one another for some time: "Stenberg and Nelson Spar to the End," "Nelson Says Attacks Called for Retaliation."

In fact, one-fifth of all headlines that mention incumbent senators by name include negative messages (see Figure 3.1). Likewise, one-fifth of headlines printed in races without incumbents contain negative phrases. Challengers are given a modest respite by editors; 16 percent of headlines mentioning challengers are negative in tone. These general averages, however, belie a great deal of variance in how papers relay negative messages to potential voters in headlines. An examination of the senate races from 1988 to 1992 indicates that in the 1990 Minnesota race between incumbent Senator Rudy Boschwitz and challenger Paul Wellstone, the Minneapolis *Star-Tribune* printed twenty-three headlines containing negative messages about Boschwitz from September 1 to election day. This represents more than one negative headline every third day. In contrast, in the same year, Senator David Boren was seeking reelection in Oklahoma against Stephan Jones. The Oklahoma City *Daily Oklahoman*, the largest circulating paper in Oklahoma, published *no* negative headlines about Boren or Jones.

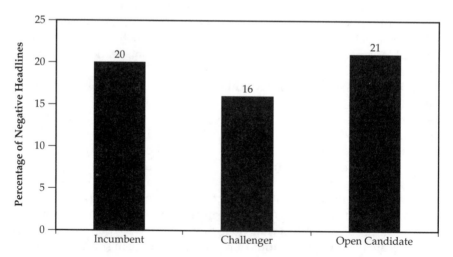

Figure 3.1   Negative Headlines Published in Newspapers

Source: Kahn and Kenney's content analysis of political advertisements (1988–1992).

For many citizens, negative headlines heighten curiosity and nudge them to read parts or all of the articles. The content of the articles is where citizens come in contact with the specific details of negative messages about the competing candidates. Generally, reporters present the specific details of negative messages in one of three ways: They print direct criticisms about the candidates; they critique the candidates' personal traits; they assess the candidates' poll standings.[3]

Pointed criticisms are often the harshest negative messages produced. Journalists routinely report criticisms of the candidates by named and unnamed sources. On average, there are fifty-three criticisms aimed directly at incumbents during the course of a campaign (see Figure 3.2).

However, similar to negative headlines, the number of criticisms varies sharply across campaigns. For example in some campaigns, as many as 300 criticisms are aimed at the incumbent during the coverage of the campaign. This translates into multiple criticisms each day of the campaign. In these races, citizens picking up a newspaper will come face to face with articles replete with criticisms. Between 1988 and 1992, Jesse Helms of North Carolina had the dubious distinction of garnering the most criticisms aimed at a U.S. senator. From September 1 to election day 1990, the Raleigh *News and Observer* printed 299 criticisms of the Republican senator. In contrast, some incumbents escape direct attacks altogether. In a small number of races contested between 1988 and 1992, newspapers printed less than ten criticisms of incumbents across the entire campaign. For example, from September 1 to election day 1990, the Anchorage *Daily News* published only five criticisms aimed at Senator Ted Stevens. Stevens received what is known in the campaign business as "a free ride" from the press.

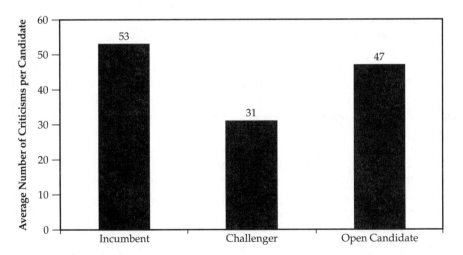

FIGURE 3.2   CRITICISMS PUBLISHED ABOUT CANDIDATE IN NEWSPAPERS

Source: Kahn and Kenney's content analysis of political advertisements (1988–1992).

Challengers, on average, receive fewer criticisms in the press, compared to incumbents and candidates in open races.[4] Challengers are the target of press criticisms, on average, thirty-one times during the length of a campaign (see Figure 3.2 on page 43). From 1988 to 1992, one-quarter of challengers were criticized less than ten times from September 1 to election day. This translates into only one criticism per week. And it is rare for the number of criticisms aimed at challengers to exceed one hundred per campaign. While challengers are criticized less than other candidates, the lack of criticisms is accompanied by a lack of press attention more generally. In other words, the press often ignore challengers completely, with reporters presenting neither negative nor positive messages about these candidates.

The most common source of criticisms in campaigns is the candidate's opponent. In fact, 20 percent of the articles written about incumbent senators contain critical comments delivered by challengers. For example, in the 2000 U.S. Senate race between Senator Rick Santorum and challenger Ron Klink, Pennsylvania newspapers often reported criticisms leveled by Santorum's challenger, Ron Klink. An article in the *Philadelphia Inquirer* on October 3 began with the headline, "Klink Tells Voters Defeating Santorum Will Improve Their Lives." The headline was only the beginning of the attack. Charges against Santorum, leveled by Klink, were reported throughout the article. Charges included: "Klink criticizes Santorum for supporting privatizing Social Security and opposing prescription drug benefit as part of Medicare," and Klink's assertion that ". . . my opponent's positions on these issues are against the interest of working Pennsylvanians."

A second common story line in negative articles centers on the unflattering descriptions of the candidates' personality traits. These are negative messages that entail the use of pejorative adjectives focusing on topics like the candidate's integrity. For example, in Ben Nelson's 1996 and 2000 campaigns, reporters focused on Nelson's "political flip-flops." In 1996, opponents charged that Governor Nelson had promised not to raise property taxes, but then he raised taxes. And in 2000, his opponents contended that he used soft money to pay for commercials early in the race, but then called for a ban on the use of soft money once his opponent was employing the same tactic. Reporters at the *World-Herald* described Nelson's behavior in these two incidents as "erratic," "inconsistent," "fuzzy," "whiney," and "opportunist," and described Nelson as a politician who "failed to keep promises." Politicians work hard to stay away from these types of descriptions.

Although challengers do not escape these sorts of descriptions, they face far fewer derogatory comments than do incumbents. On average, incumbents and candidates in open races run into approximately twenty attacks on their personal traits per campaign (see Figure 3.3). Challengers, on the other hand, receive about half as many attacks on their personal character. One of the most common criticisms leveled against challengers in the news is the description of the challenger as a "political neophyte."

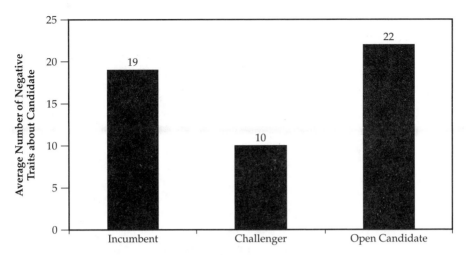

FIGURE 3.3 **NEGATIVE TRAITS PUBLISHED ABOUT CANDIDATE IN NEWSPAPERS**

Source: Kahn and Kenney's content analysis of political advertisements (1988–1992).

Again, the variance in trait criticisms is impressive. For example, between 1988 and 1992 the number of negative traits aimed at senators in the largest circulating newspapers across the nation ranged from zero to seventy-seven. When Senator Joe Lieberman challenged controversial Senator Lowell We-icker in Connecticut in 1988, the *Hartford Courant* helped Lieberman's candidacy by printing seventy-seven criticisms of Weicker's personal traits. In stark contrast, newspapers in four states during the 1988–1992 period published no negative trait references about the incumbent senators running for reelection. The fortunate senators included Bob Graham of Florida, Nancy Kassebaum of Kansas, Harry Reid of Nevada, and Dale Bumpers of Arkansas. Although the average number of personal attacks on challengers is less than half that of incumbents, over ten percent of challengers faced over thirty criticisms aimed at their personal traits during their campaigns. This number of criticisms translates into more than one every other day.

A final technique used by writers to convey negative information about a candidate is to present details about the candidates' standings in public opinion polls. Voters consider the candidates' poll standings when deciding whom to support.[5] For example, results of polls detailing the challenger's inability to increase support among potential voters often produce negative images of the challenger. Although Ben Nelson's inability to hold leads in the polls formed the basis of many stories in the *World-Herald* in mid-October of both campaigns, challengers receive the most negative coverage when it comes to poll standings. An article published in the *Albuquerque Journal* about the U.S. Senate race between Democratic incumbent Jeff Bingaman and challenger Bill Redmond illustrates how horse-race coverage can generate critical coverage of the trailing candidate. The newspaper reports the results of a recent poll showing that

> New Mexico voters support Democrat incumbent Jeff Bingaman by a more than 2-to-1 margin in a U.S. Senate race against Republican Bill Redmond. "Jeff Bingaman is ahead of Bill Redmond by 29 points. That's a sizable lead," said Research and Polling Inc.'s Brian Sanderoff. "Even if every one of the undecided went to Redmond, Bingaman still would be ahead."

From 1988 to 1992, we examined each story about poll standings in the largest circulating papers in all states and scored the stories on a scale ranging from one to five. Stories that contained a positive spin on poll standings received a 5 (e.g., the candidate is way ahead and appears to be increasing his or her lead); stories that discussed poll standings in neutral language were scored a 3 (e.g., the candidate remains approximately 12–15 points behind— the same percentage as three weeks ago); and stories that were negative about poll numbers received a 1 (e.g., the candidate is so far behind it appears his or her campaign is hopeless).

Most stories about incumbents were positive in tone, receiving an average score of 4.1 (see Figure 3.4). This is not the case for challengers. Most stories about challengers tended to be negative in tone, receiving an average rating of 2.0. And horse-race coverage of open race candidates was more favorable than horse-race coverage of challengers, yet less favorable than coverage of incumbents (i.e., an average of 3.0).

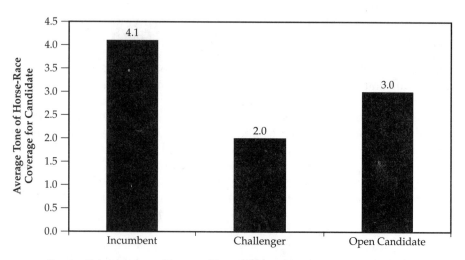

FIGURE 3.4   AVERAGE TONE OF HORSE-RACE COVERAGE IN NEWSPAPERS

Source: Kahn and Kenney's content analysis of political advertisements (1988–1992).

Of course, incumbents do not completely escape negative coverage of their poll standings. When incumbents find themselves in a competitive race, reporters often focus on the incumbents' troubles. After all, it is compelling news when incumbents are on the precipice of losing their jobs. For example, Senator Slade Gorton was locked in a competitive battle with challenger Marie Cantwell in Washington in the fall of 2000. Gorton was seeking his third consecutive term. He had won in 1994 by 10 percentage points. Nonetheless, two polls conducted in late October of 2000 indicated the race was very close. Papers throughout the state were reporting the latest polls. A story in a Seattle paper began with the headline "Gorton-Cantwell Race Close." Within the first two lines of the story, the author, Joel Connelly, notes the incumbent's troubles:

> Senator Slade Gorton enjoys a tiny lead over Democratic challenger Maria Cantwell as Washington's hotly contested U.S. Senate race goes into its final two weeks, according to a pair of new statewide polls of Washington voters. In both surveys, however, the Republican senator (i.e., Gorton) polls well short of 50 percent, which many opinion experts consider a danger sign for incumbents.

It turns out that "opinion experts" were correct, barely, as Gorton lost his senate seat in an extremely close race: Cantwell 48.72 percent to Gorton 48.64 percent.

In the end, headlines and criticisms of various sorts combine to create a general tone for news articles. It is the overall tone that most likely remains with voters, rather than specific criticisms or detailed poll numbers. On average, then, how often do negative articles appear in newspapers during a campaign season? For incumbents, 12 percent of the articles appearing in newspapers from September 1 to election day were negative; for candidates in open races, the percentage increases to 15; and for challengers the percentage increases again to 17 (see Figure 3.5 on page 48). As with all the analyses thus far in this chapter, there is considerable variance on the number of negative articles about the candidates. For example, in the 1988–1992 senate races, the number of negative articles about incumbents ranged from zero (i.e., Senator Al Gore of Tennessee in 1990) to fifty-six (i.e., Senator Jesse Helms of North Carolina).

It is clear, then, that voters experience negative messages via the press in various ways. The simplest and most straightforward message is the headline. Beyond the headline, reporters and editors deliver the details of the negative information in the body of the articles they write and print. Yet there is dramatic variation in the amount and tone of the negativity produced by the press. As we have seen, in some campaigns there is a dearth of negative information; whereas, in other campaigns negative messages are pervasive. Why is the variance so dramatic? Coming to grips with this question will move us toward understanding why some voters cannot escape scathing negative attacks of candidates, while other voters go about reading the paper and never bump into a negative headline or article about the candidates.

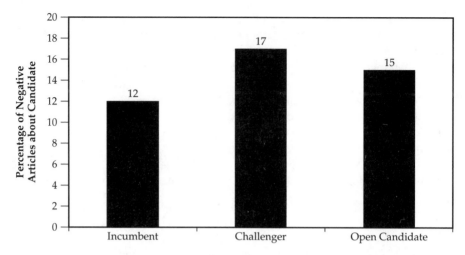

FIGURE 3.5   NEGATIVE ARTICLES PUBLISHED IN NEWSPAPERS

Source: Kahn and Kenney's content analysis of political advertisements (1988–1992).

EXPLAINING THE VARIANCE
IN THE AMOUNT OF NEGATIVITY IN THE PRESS

To understand the variations in the tone of news coverage, we look at three sets of factors: (1) the candidates' strategies; (2) the political context; and (3) the characteristics of the candidates.[6] These forces should explain why some races experience a great deal of negative coverage while others witness nary a cross word in the press.

We begin with the behavior and strategies of the candidates themselves. Press coverage is likely to be more negative if the candidates are running attack ads and are criticizing each other in stump speeches and in debates. The press are likely to describe these political communications when covering campaigns, thereby producing critical coverage of the sparring candidates. The U.S. press have several incentives to relay negative information from the candidates to citizens. One important incentive is to sell newspapers. Because there are only two senators from each state, stories about senators and their challengers are of interest to the papers' readers. And the public's interest may be heightened when the candidates are exchanging criticisms of one another. A second reason papers echo the candidates' messages is because reporters and editors feel they have an obligation to pass along campaign information to readers, since an important function of newspapers is to relay information from political elites to the newspaper's readers.[7]

An example of the press's mirroring of the candidates' attacks comes from an article appearing in the *Burlington Free Press* on October 9, 2000. In the U.S Senate race between Senator James Jeffords and challenger Edward Flanagan,

Flanagan, while on the campaign trail, repeatedly criticized Jefford's record. The headline of an article on October 9th read, "Flanagan rips Jeffords on Drug Re-importation Bill." The article begins,

> U.S. Senate candidate Edward Flanagan on Monday sharply criticized incumbent Sen. James Jeffords for "caving in to the big drug companies on a bill to allow U.S.-made drugs to be re-imported into the country. The outcome of the drug re-importation bill shows what's wrong with Washington and how Jim Jeffords style of governing is failing Vermonters," Flanagan said.

In other contests where the competing candidates are emphasizing their own issue stands and personal qualifications, coverage is often less critical. For example, during the 2000 U.S. Senate race in North Dakota between Senator Kent Conrad and Republican challenger Duane Sand, both candidates focused on their own issue positions, especially agriculture. An article published in the *Bismarck Tribune* on September 14 describes Sand's farm policy. The article begins, "North Dakota's Republican candidate for the U.S. Senate . . . proposed seven tools to remedy the ailing national farm policy. Sand claimed his program would double commodity prices within 10 years." The article continues by detailing the specific tools recommended by Sand such as "support for value-added agriculture ventures with low-interest loans and grants, tax credits, and tax reform." The article lacks any criticisms of the opponent's views and simply articulates the challenger's policy agenda, thereby producing a positive article.

Similarly, Sand's opponent, Senator Kent Conrad, focused on his policy views and achievements, rarely criticizing his opponent. Conrad's coverage in the *Bismarck Tribune* reflected this strategy. For example, in an article published on October 15th, Conrad uses a campaign appearance to draw attention to his ability to capture "record federal disaster payments to help North Dakota farmers through difficult times. . . . Conrad also points to congressional action on . . . legislation as a sign of progress for North Dakota's water project. 'This bill represents years of hard work, and several months of tough negotiations with our friends in the downstream states,' Conrad said Friday." The article in the *Bismarck Tribune* echoes Conrad's campaign rhetoric, highlighting Conrad's achievements and "hard work" in the U.S. Senate.

While the candidates' own campaign messages may influence the tone of coverage, characteristics of the campaign environment may also affect the negativity of press coverage. Press coverage becomes increasingly negative as races become more hard-fought.[8] In competitive races, newspapers are more likely to cover the contests in more detail, since the campaigns are more exciting and more interesting to readers. Also, as we saw in Chapter 2, candidates are more likely to attack each other as races become more negative, and these attacks are viewed as especially newsworthy in tight races.

Another factor influencing the amount of negative press coverage is the time period of the campaign. During the early days of campaigns (i.e., September), coverage may be more positive, as newspapers introduce the candidates to their readers. As election day approaches, press coverage may become more negative. Coverage of the campaign may also become more negative during the final days simply because candidates rely more heavily on negative messages during the final weeks of the campaign (see Chapter 2).

Finally, the characteristics of the candidates may influence the amount of negativity in the news.[9] For instance, when examining negative coverage of incumbents, it may be the case that senior senators, with long tenures in the U.S. Senate and secure ties with the local press, may be less likely to receive negative coverage, especially compared to more junior senators. In addition, quality challengers may be more effective at generating critical coverage of sitting senators, compared to challengers with less experience, less skill, and less resources.

Similarly, the gender of the candidate may influence the tone of coverage. Female senatorial candidates typically received more negative coverage compared to male candidates.[10] Much of the negative coverage is focused on the female candidates' lack of viability.

THE POWER OF COMPETITION AND CANDIDATE BEHAVIOR

To examine how the candidates' strategies, the campaign environment, and the characteristics of the candidates influence the tone of coverage, we look at the measures of negative press attention introduced earlier: the overall tone of the articles written about the candidates; the tone of the headlines; the number of criticisms published about the candidates; the number of negative traits written about the candidates; the tone of the horse race.[11]

The central finding that emerges from the analysis is that the closeness of the race consistently influences every aspect of negative coverage for incumbents and challengers (see Table 3.1). However, the effect of competition varies across incumbents and challengers.[12] For incumbents, the competitiveness of the race always increases negative coverage. In contrast, for challengers, increases in competition yield mixed results. For some measures of tone, challengers in close races receive more positive coverage than their less competitive counterparts, while other measures of tone produce more critical coverage of competitive challengers.

We begin by focusing on the three measures of negativity where the effects of competition are opposite for incumbents and challengers. As races become more competitive, the tone of articles, the tone of headlines, and the tone of horse-race coverage become more negative for incumbents. In contrast, challengers in competitive races receive more positive articles, more positive headlines, and more favorable horse-race coverage, compared to challengers in less competitive contests (see Table 3.1).

TABLE 3.1 EXPLAINING THE NEGATIVITY OF PRESS COVERAGE

A. TONE OF COVERAGE FOR INCUMBENTS

	OVERALL TONE	HEADLINE TONE	CRITICISMS	TRAITS	HORSE RACE
Incumbent Negativity	−.68 (.21)***	−.43 (.21)**	30.35 (9.56)***	.12 (4.68)	−.04 (.12)
Challenger Negativity	−.17 (.20)	−.04(.20)	5.66 (9.64)	4.35 (4.72)	.07 (.12)
Competition	−.02 (.006)***	−.02 (.006)***	.90 (.28)***	.42 (.14)***	−.02 (.003)***
Incumbent Spending	−1.58 (1.14)	−1.60 (1.16)	37.50 (53.40)	−2.58 (26.18)	1.12 (.67)*
Challenger Spending	−32 (1.56)	−1.34 (1.58)	87.09 (73.13)	59.59 (35.85)	−1.62 (.92)*
Open Race	.18 (.28)	.06 (.28)	3.34 (13.37)	3.80 (6.56)	.03 (.16)
Seniority	.004 (.01)	.007 (.01)	.89 (.58)	.15 (.28)	.004 (.008)
Gender	−.28 (.21)	−.32 (.21)	10.95 (9.42)	1.20 (4.61)	.008 (.12)
Challenger Quality	.01 (.03)	.02 (.03)	−1.93 (1.22)	−.83 (.60)	.0007 (.01)
Week of Campaign	−.35 (.43)	−.41 (.43)	10.03 (19.10)	10.10 (9.36)	−.23 (.25)
Governor's Race	—	—	−23.96 (8.88)***	−5.71 (4.35)	—
Presidential Year	—	—	12.29 (9.94)	3.83 (4.87)	—
Size of Newspaper	—	—	.007 (.003)**	.0002 (.001)	—
Constant	2.53 (.60)***	2.68 (.61)***	−77.98 (28.99)***	−36.92 (14.21)**	6.06 (.35)***
R^2	.45	.42	.51	.39	.55
N	96	96	96	96	96

B. TONE OF COVERAGE FOR CHALLENGERS

	OVERALL TONE	HEADLINE TONE	CRITICISMS	TRAITS	HORSE RACE
Incumbent Negativity	.06 (.06)	−.04 (.06)	17.11 (5.53)***	.27 (3.55)	.02 (.12)
Challenger Negativity	−.09 (.05)*	−07 (.06)	3.89 (5.58)	7.21 (3.58)**	.00008 (.12)
Competition	.006 (.002)***	.004 (.002)**	.75 (.16)***	.25 (.10)**	.02 (.003)***
Incumbent Spending	−.26 (.31)	−.02 (.36)	−16.59 (30.93)	−16.85 (19.82)	−.70 (.68)
Challenger Spending	.21 (.43)	.93 (.49)*	41.08 (42.34)	5.55 (27.15)	1.67 (.93)*
Open Race	−.15 (.08)*	−.12 (.09)	.51 (7.74)	5.24 (4.96)	−.10 (.17)
Seniority	−.007 (.003)*	−.005 (.004)	.30 (.34)	.01 (.22)	−.007 (.008)
Gender	.06 (.06)	.17 (.06)***	−1.50 (5.45)	−5.57 (3.49)	−.03 (.12)
Challenger Quality	.006 (.007)	.009 (.008)	−1.22 (.71)*	−.01 (.45)	.001 (.02)
Week of Campaign	.04 (.12)	.10 (.13)	−2.68 (11.06)	−8.28 (7.09)	.24 (.25)
Governor's Race	—	—	−10.20 (5.15)*	−2.38 (3.30)	—
Presidential Year	—	—	2.07 (5.76)	1.92 (3.69)	—
Size of Newspaper	—	—	.005 (.002)**	.003 (.001)***	—
Constant	−.51 (.16)***	−.44 (.19)**	−47.29 (16.79)***	−12.05 (10.76)	.13 (.36)
R^2	.28	.23	.58	.36	.51
N	96	96	96	96	96

Tone of coverage is the average tone score for all articles mainly about the candidate during the campaign. Tone of headline coverage is the average tone score for all headlines mentioning the candidate during the campaign. Criticisms is the number of criticisms published about the candidate during the campaign. Tone of trait coverage is the number of negative traits published about the candidate during the campaign. Tone of horse-race coverage is the average viability score based on all the articles written about the candidate. See Appendix A for information about the operationalization of independent variables. In each cell, we present the unstandardized OLS regression coefficient with the standard error (in parentheses).

All p-values are two-tailed.

***$p < .01$

**$p < .05$

*$p < .10$

In addition, the impact of competition on coverage is greater for incumbents than challengers. For example, the size of the coefficient predicting the impact of competition on tone of articles is –.02 for incumbents and .006 for challengers. Therefore, the influence of competition on coverage is over three times more powerful for incumbents than for challengers. We find the same pattern for the tone of headline coverage (i.e., –.02 for incumbents and .004 for challengers). In the case of headlines, the impact of competition is five times more powerful for incumbents than for challengers.

Why do incumbents in tight races receive more negative coverage than challengers in similar contests? One possibility is that some of the negative coverage aimed at incumbents focuses on viability. For example, during Senator Conrad Burns reelection campaign in Montana, the newspapers spent plenty of time focusing on challenger Brian Schweitzer's improvements in local polls and Burns's corresponding decline in support. An article published at the end of September, with the headline "Burns still leads, but Schweitzer closing the gap," detailed the results of a recent poll. The lead sentence of the article explains, "Republican Sen. Conrad Burns continues to lead his Democratic challenger, but Brian Schweitzer has closed the gap considerably in the past four months, according to a recent poll. . . . The poll shows that Burns's lead has been cut in half since May."

Another possibility is that negative coverage of competitive incumbents focuses on the incumbents' tenure in office. Incumbents who find themselves in hard-fought races may have poor records of performance as senators. Vulnerable incumbents may have taken controversial or inconsistent stands on issues, or they may be viewed as inattentive to their constituents. For example, during Senator Charles Robb's 2000 reelection campaign against challenger George F. Allen, media coverage criticized Robb's record as a U.S. senator. An article published in the *Virginian-Pilot* on November 2, 2000 began as follows:

> Looking to bolster support among service members and veterans, challenger George F. Allen lashed back at Sen. Charles S. Robb Wednesday, saying the senator has had an inconsistent record on military issues. Allen cited Robb's record on several defense bills, including a 1997 vote that could have meant an additional $20 million to accelerate improvements to the Norfolk Naval Shipyard.

While competitive races bring about negative coverage of incumbents and positive coverage of challengers in some areas of the newspaper (i.e., tone of article, tone of headlines, tone of horse-race coverage), the divergent effects of competition disappear when we examine other areas of coverage (i.e., the number of criticisms, the number of negative personal traits). Competition increases the number of criticisms published about incumbents *and* challengers.[13] For example, incumbents who have safe leads in the polls (i.e., the incumbent is fifty points ahead of the challenger) experience approximately forty five fewer criticisms in the press, compared to incumbents who are in races with uncertain outcomes.[14]

The increase in criticisms due to competition is illustrated in the press treatment of the neck-and-neck race between Maria Cantwell and Senator Slade Gorton of Washington. In the final days of the campaign, a Seattle newspaper ran a story with the headline "Fiery Final Debate for Senate; Cantwell, Gorton Attack Each Other on Radio Show." The article reads,

> GOP Sen. Slade Gorton went on the attack in a radio debate yesterday, accusing Democratic challenger Maria Cantwell of breathtaking hypocrisy in calling for campaign finance reform and a parents be damned attitude on abortion notification. Cantwell returned the fire, saying Gorton has made charges he knows are untrue about Democrats' plans for prescription drug coverage under Medicare, and has given preferential treatment to special interests in Washington, D.C.

Competition also increases the chances that negative personal traits will be mentioned in the coverage of incumbents *and* challengers. In competitive races, incumbents are more likely to be called erratic, out of touch, or tied to the negative aspects of the Washington establishment (e.g., strong relationships with large money contributors). Incumbents in close races can expect, on average, twenty additional attacks on their characters, compared to incumbents who lead by large margins. Similarly, competitive challengers receive more negative trait references than their noncompetitive colleagues. In the press, competitive challengers are sometimes referred to as "inexperienced," as "carpetbaggers," as "uninformed," and "hypocritical."

While competition has a powerful influence on the tone of coverage for both incumbents and challengers, the tone of the candidates' messages also has an impact on coverage. As candidates become more negative, media coverage becomes more negative. However, compared to the relationship between competition and coverage, the relationship between candidate behavior and coverage is less consistent and less intuitive. When incumbents attack their opponents they expect their criticisms to appear in the coverage of challengers. And, obviously, when challengers attack incumbents, they hope that reporters and editors reprint their criticisms. These straightforward expectations by the candidates, however, do not often materialize. We turn first to an examination of coverage when the incumbents go negative.

Incumbents influence only one type of challenger press coverage when they conduct negative campaigns. They increase the number of press criticisms published about their challengers. In particular, when incumbents criticize challengers, the press prints, on average, an additional seventeen criticisms aimed directly at challengers, compared to races where incumbents are not criticizing challengers.

However, incumbents who "go negative" also increase the amount of negative coverage about their own candidacies. Specifically, when incumbents are critical of challengers, the tone of articles and headlines about themselves becomes more negative. In addition, the number of direct criticisms aimed at incumbents increases when senators criticize challengers. Specifically, when incumbents criticize challengers, they generate, on average, thirty more criticisms in the press aimed at their own campaigns, compared to incumbents who refrain from criticizing challengers. In fact, when incumbents criticize challengers, they generate more criticisms in the press of themselves than they do of their challengers.

Challengers fare even worse when they use negative strategies. When challengers attack incumbents, they fail to influence the tone of incumbents' coverage at all. Challengers' attacks appear to be in vain. Reporters and editors ignore their attacks altogether and do not alter the press treatment of incumbents. And, similar to incumbents, challengers on the attack hurt their own coverage. Indeed, the tone of articles about challengers becomes more negative and the number of negative traits printed about challengers increases when challengers engage in negative campaigning.

So, in the end, the strategies used by incumbents and challengers to encourage negative coverage of the opposition are far less effective than candidates would hope. In fact, in several cases their negative strategies backfire, instigating more negative coverage of their own candidacies. These relationships persist even when we control for a variety of rival explanations including the closeness of the race, the quality of the challenger, and the amount of spending by the candidates.[15]

The 2000 race between incumbent Rod Grams and challenger Mark Dayton provides an example of how Grams's attack strategy often generated negative coverage of his own candidacy. The article with the headline "Grams Steps Up Attack on Dayton" illustrates how Grams's negative strategy was more effective at producing critical coverage of his own campaign than increasing negative coverage of Dayton.

> According to Dayton's communications director, Sharon Ruhland, "The overall message is that Grams is desperate. He knows that Mark Dayton has done a wonderful job of connecting with voters, and he's taking anything he can find and distorting it, twisting it." . . . Dayton is trying to capitalize on Grams's attacks, running a TV commercial that appeals to voters to reject what he says is Grams's style of negative politics.

Why does negative campaigning by candidates encourage negative press coverage of their *own* candidacies? A possible explanation has to do with the so-called media "backlash." In our interviews with campaign managers, strategists often worried that when candidates decided to attack their opponents, critical press coverage of their own candidates would escalate. Indeed, voters often develop negative images of candidates who attack their opponents.[16] The press, like voters, may also dislike negative campaign techniques and may demonstrate their displeasure in their coverage.

Furthermore, over the past decade, the press has begun to systematically examine the content of negative appeals. The press spends space and time analyzing the accuracy, credibility, and relevance of the attacks. Newspapers are especially aggressive when attacks appear pejorative, ad hominem in nature, or unrelated to governing. In other words, reporters may produce more coverage examining a candidate's charge than they do printing the original accusation. This was the case in Nelson's 1996 campaign against now Senator Hagel. Nelson focused on Hagel's actions as the president of a highly successful cellular telephone business. Nelson claimed in an ad that Hagel, "was in apparent violation of the law" during some business dealings with the federal government. Hagel aggressively defended his actions. The Omaha *World-Herald* began to investigate. Nelson's attacks became the focus of press criticisms, rather than Hagel's business practices. A story on October 27, 1996, produced a harsh critique of Nelson.

> Hagel's business record was the subject of a story by this newspaper's Paul Goodsell last spring. The reporter found no wrongdoing. Nor did the Federal Communications Commission, which had received and investigated a complaint (against Hagel). But Nelson, using words like "fraud" and "rigging," is trying to deceive Nebraskans into thinking that Chuck Hagel is untrustworthy. The governor's efforts to take the spotlight off state tax and spending matters cannot change the facts. If the governor thinks that stooping to unsubstantiated personal attacks will enhance his campaigns, he's wrong.

This kind of analysis by the *World-Herald* is commonplace in newspapers today. In fact, during the 1990s, the press began to systematically analyze candidates' commercials. Newspapers coined this type of coverage "ad watches." We turn now to a detailed examination of ad watches. By using these "ad watches," reporters and editors are actively, forcefully at times, monitoring and checking candidates' messages for truth and accuracy. Clearly, if successful, the press is performing an important task for distracted citizens trying to sort out what is true and false in the candidates' advertising. Citizen's costs of gathering accurate information would decrease sharply if they could pick up their local paper and quickly assess the veracity of the candidates' claims.

"AD WATCHES" IN THE PRESS: CRITIQUING THE CANDIDATES' COMMERCIALS

Ad watches appeared in 52 percent of the races in the newspapers examined in this study. They were less prominent in 1988; only 40 percent of the newspapers conducted the watches. But by 1992, 67 percent of the newspapers were running ad watches during campaigns. By 2000, ad watches had become a staple of modern political reporting. What factors encourage or suppress the publication of ad watches?

Ad watches tend to appear in three specific circumstances (see Figure 3.6). First, the closeness of the race influences the prevalence of ad watches. When newspapers are covering competitive contests, over forty paragraphs assessing the candidates' advertisements appear in the newspaper. In contrast, when newspapers are covering noncompetitive campaigns, a meager fourteen paragraphs are devoted to analyses of the candidates' commercials.[17] Secondly, the professionalism of the newspaper also influences the newspaper's propensity to assess the candidates' advertisements. Newspapers with larger staffs and more space to print the news are more likely to publish ad watches. In fact, in large newspapers, twenty-five paragraphs are devoted to analysis of the candidates' advertisements during the campaign, compared to twelve paragraphs in small newspapers.[18]

Finally, newspapers seem responsive to the candidates' campaign strategies. When candidates engage in negative campaigning, newspapers respond by conducting more ad watches. For example, when both candidates run negative campaigns, newspapers devote an average of forty paragraphs to analyzing the candidates' commercials. In contrast, when both candidates refrain from negative campaigning, only seven paragraphs are published during the course of the campaign assessing the accuracy of the candidates' advertisements.

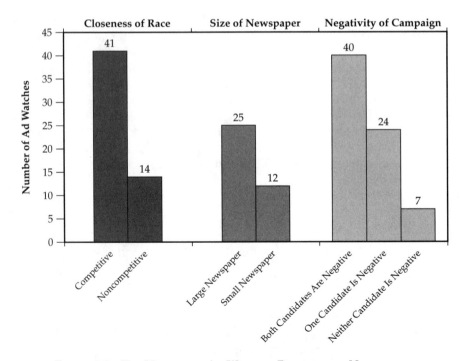

FIGURE 3.6   THE NUMBER OF AD WATCHES PUBLISHED IN NEWSPAPERS

Source: Kahn and Kenney's content analysis of newspaper coverage (1988–1992).

When newspapers decide to publish ad watches, what do reporters write about when assessing the candidates' ads? Reporters tend to describe commercials in one of three ways: containing "accurate" information, containing "both accurate and inaccurate" information, or containing "wholly inaccurate" information. Most candidate advertisements are viewed as containing at least some inaccuracies (see Figure 3.7). In fact, only 24 percent of the incumbent commercials, 21 percent of the challenger commercials, and 17 percent of the commercials in open races are considered "accurate" portrayals of the facts. Many commercials contain accurate statements alongside untrue statements. For example, 40 percent of all commercials contain both "accurate" and "inaccurate" information about the candidates. However, 39 percent of all ads assessed by the media are considered containing *only* inaccurate information.

To illustrate, an ad watch published during the 2000 New Jersey campaign for the U.S. Senate in the *Newark Star-Ledger* examines an advertisement by Democrat Jon Corzine that criticized his opponent, Bob Franks, for absenteeism in Congress. The commercial begins,

> Congressman Bob Franks. He just missed 29 straight votes in Congress. He missed a crucial vote to toughen the drunk driving laws, missed another one to crack down on hate crimes. . . . He even missed a vote on safety standards to prevent gas pipeline explosions like the one in Edison a few years ago. Bob Franks. He's being paid by the taxpayers but he's not showing up for work.

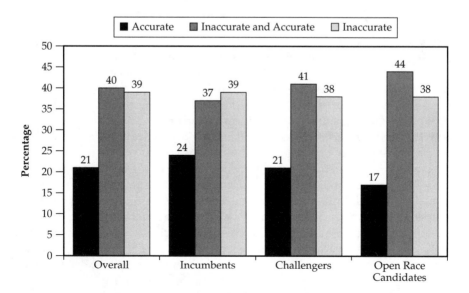

FIGURE 3.7   THE ASSESSMENT OF ADS IN "AD WATCHES"

Source: Kahn and Kenney's content analysis of news coverage (1988–1992).

In the ad watch, the reporter acknowledges that Franks missed votes during his busy campaign. Nonetheless, his overall attendance record is 99 percent during his eight years in Congress. The reporter goes on to say that the absences described in the commercial are documented, but the significance of the measures are exaggerated, especially on the pipeline safety issue. While the advertisement claims the bill would improve safety, in actuality, safety advocates opposed the bill and applauded its defeat. Franks, who worked on the issue, missed the vote because he was delayed in traffic. Franks says he would have voted "no." New Jerseys' twelve other representatives all voted "no."

This ad watch, like many others, presents the text of the candidate's commercial, and then assesses the accuracy of the statements presented in the advertisement. The reporter summarizing the Corzine commercial believes the advertisement includes some factually correct statements. However, the reporter also points out that many of the details are presented in a misleading and exaggerated fashion.

In the next example we present an ad watch in which reporters determined that the candidate's ad contained no accurate information. The ad watch appeared on the second page of the Metro section of the *Minneapolis Star Tribune* during the 2000 U.S. Senate campaign. As usual, the article begins with a description of the advertisement:

> It's crazy. Mark Dayton's schemes. He's called for increased spending on 41 different programs. . . . His plans are risky and reckless. . . . What's really scary is his health care plan. It'll cost every Minnesotan $142 more for their health insurance. The Congressional Budget Office says Dayton's plan would result in a million Americans losing health coverage. Higher costs, less coverage, that's the scary truth behind Mark Dayton's schemes.

Following the description of the text of the commercial, the reporter begins her analysis by saying, "The ad is inaccurate and misleading on several accounts." The reporter points out that the Congressional Budget Office (CBO) has never examined Dayton's health plan. Furthermore, because the CBO has not examined Dayton's plan, "it's also wrong to say that the CBO says Dayton's plan would result in a million Americans losing health coverage." Finally, the reporter explains that it is misleading to attach a specific dollar figure to a plan that has never been "costed out."

We turn to one last inquiry concerning ad watches: Are newspapers more likely to describe candidates' advertisements as inaccurate during negative campaigns? We think so. Reporters may be more likely to investigate negative commercials because these commercials contain criticisms and harsh accusations of opponents. Put simply, negative commercials are more newsworthy than positive ads. In addition, it is easier to check the accuracy of specific accusations (e.g., as discussed earlier—Franks' absenteeism on floor votes), compared to assertions made in positive commercials (e.g., candidate Hillary Clinton's claim, in her 2000 New York campaign, that she cares about the people of New York).

Finally, the press may view negative commercials as potentially more damaging to candidates than positive commercials; therefore, reporters may spend more time ascertaining the accuracy of negative charges. This belief emerged during the 1988 presidential election between Vice President George Bush and Governor of Massachusetts Michael Dukakis. Bush aired a series of hard-hitting advertisements criticizing Dukakis. The press, by and large, did not dissect the veracity of the negative advertisements. After Bush's victory, many reporters regretted their lack of vigilance and vowed to be more watchful in the future.[19] If reporters are spending more time examining the accuracy of negative commercials, they may be more successful in uncovering erroneous statements in negative advertisements, especially compared to positive advertisements.

While candidates' negative messages may influence the substance of the assessments offered by reporters, other characteristics of the race may also contribute to reporters' evaluations of ads. For instance, candidates in competitive races are more likely to air negative advertisements. Thus, the press may be more likely to point out the distortions in advertisements displayed in competitive races. In addition, negative commercials become more prevalent in the last few days of campaigns. Reporters, then, may be more likely to discuss the inaccuracies in advertisements late in the campaign. Furthermore, candidates may become more desperate near the end of the campaign and may be more willing to air advertisements with more distortions close to election day.

We analyze the assessments of candidates' ads made by reporters and editors in Table 3.2 on page 60.[20] Beginning with assessments of incumbent advertisements, the tone of incumbents' campaigns influence evaluations made by the press.[21] Incumbents who engage in negative campaigning can expect reporters to view their commercials as less accurate than those of incumbents who run positive campaigns.

The closeness of the race also influences the types of assessments made by reporters in their ad watches.[22] As races become more competitive, reporters become more critical in their assessments of the incumbents' advertisements. Similarly, the timing of commercials influences the type of evaluations made by reporters. In particular, as election day approaches, reporters are more likely to view the incumbents' advertisements as containing errors, compared to advertisements aired earlier in the campaign season.

Turning to challengers' advertisements, the tone of the candidates' campaigns does not influence assessments of the challengers' advertisements. Challengers who "go negative" are not viewed by the press as less accurate in their ads, compared to challengers who "stay positive." And, unlike incumbents, the competitiveness of the races does not influence how reporters assess the commercials of challengers.

However, the timing of the commercials continues to influence the reporters' assessments of the challengers' commercials. Similar to incumbents, as election day approaches, ad watches are more likely to conclude that the

TABLE 3.2   EXPLAINING NEWSPAPERS' ASSESSMENTS OF ADS

	ASSESSMENTS OF INCUMBENTS' ADS
	UNSTANDARDIZED OLS COEFFICIENT (STANDARD ERROR)
Incumbent Negativity	.06 (.02)***
Challenger Negativity	−.03(.02)
Competition	.001 (.0005)***
Open Race	.04 (.01)***
Week of Campaign	.12 (.04)***
Constant	−.17 (.05)***
R^2	.34
N	96

	ASSESSMENTS OF CHALLENGERS' ADS
	UNSTANDARDIZED OLS COEFFICIENT (STANDARD ERROR)
Incumbent Negativity	.02 (.02)
Challenger Negativity	.005(.02)
Competition	.0007 (.0007)
Open Race	.04 (.01)***
Week of Campaign	.09 (.03)***
Constant	−.12 (.05)***
R^2	.26
N	96

The dependent variable is the average "ad watch" assessment in each race.
See Appendix A for information about the operationalization of the independent variables.
All p-values are two-tailed.
*** $p < .01$
** $p < .05$
* $p < .10$

challengers' commercials contain factual errors, compared to ad watches published earlier in the campaign. Finally, the type of race has an impact on the
content of the ad watches. Challengers are viewed as producing more accurate advertisements, compared to candidates who eventually lose open races.
Similarly, incumbents are seen as running more truthful commercials than
winners in open races.

SUMMARY

This chapter examined how newspapers cover negative messages in U.S. Senate campaigns. Articles containing negative messages vary dramatically across
campaigns. In some papers, in some years, stories are replete with negative

messages every day of the campaign. At other times, negative stories are rare. In some races, not a single negative story is published during the entire length of the campaign.

Why the dramatic variance? We find support for two explanations: (1) the level of competitiveness in the race, and (2) differences in the behavior of the candidates. Newspapers spend a great deal of time reporting negative messages in competitive races, especially compared to contests where polls indicate one candidate has a commanding lead. Since competitive races are more interesting to readers, newspaper editors dedicate more resources to the coverage of these races. More reporters are assigned to these contests and more newspaper space is allocated to the coverage of competitive campaigns. Similarly, since the outcome of these races are uncertain, reporters and editors may feel an obligation to scrutinize the candidates more carefully. Claims by the candidates are likely to be examined more systematically, the background of the candidates may be evaluated more closely, and the strategies of the candidates may be studied more thoroughly.

Although competition consistently influences the tone of coverage, the influence of candidate behavior on press coverage is less straightforward. We found when candidates criticize their opponents, the press actually presents more negative coverage of the attacking candidates. Although candidates have multiple objectives when attacking their opponents, they clearly do not intend to generate negative coverage of their own candidacies. But, indeed, they do. This appears to be the price of disseminating negative messages. There is a media "backlash," as feared by political strategists.

Finally, we examined the contemporary phenomenon known as "ad watches." In senate campaigns, reporters and editors are taking time to assess the accuracy and fairness of the candidates' claims in their commercials. Journalists report findings from their research in well-publicized and prominently displayed ad watches. These articles are more prevalent in larger newspapers, in competitive races, and in campaigns where the candidates have decided to air "attack" ads. In addition, the content of the ad watches varies with the closeness of the race and the strategies of the candidates. For instance, when evaluating the advertisements of incumbents' commercials, reporters are more likely to view advertisements as inaccurate if senators are running in close races and if they are airing negative advertisements.

In summary, although negative campaigning does not characterize all campaigns for the U.S. Senate, once candidates engage in negative messages the news media pick up on the negativity and begin to relay the negative messages to potential voters. The voters' political environment becomes inundated with candidates' charges and countercharges. In turn, these accusations are replayed in the press. In the end, some voters are saturated with negative messages, while other voters never see or hear a cross word from the candidates or the press. This dramatic difference in the voters' campaign environments undoubtedly influences citizens' levels of information about the candidates and their assessments of the competing candidates. We turn now to an examination of how differences in the amount and type of negative campaign messages influence citizens' views of the candidates and the campaign.

NOTES

1. For a detailed discussion of the 1996 campaign, see Doug McAuliff, "Cornhusker Upset: Underdog Defeats Nebraska's Popular Governor in 1996 Senate Race," in *Campaign and Elections: Contemporary Case Studies*, ed. Michael A. Bailey, Ronald A. Faucheux, Paul S. Herrnson, and Clyde Wilcox (Washington D.C.: Congressional Quarterly Press, 2000).
2. Kim F. Kahn. "Senate Elections in the News: An Examination of the Characteristics and Determinants of Campaign Coverage," *Legislative Studies Quarterly* 16 (1991): 349–374.
3. Kim F. Kahn and Patrick J. Kenney, *The Spectacle of U.S. Senate Campaigns* (Princeton, NJ: Princeton University Press, 1999).
4. Candidates in open races receive nearly as many criticisms as incumbents.
5. Larry M. Bartels, *Presidential Primaries and the Dynamics of Public Choice* (Princeton, NJ: Princeton University Press, 1988).
6. Peter Clark and Susan Evans, *Covering Campaigns: Journalism in Congressional Elections* (Stanford, CA: Stanford University Press, 1983); Kim F. Kahn and Patrick J. Kenney. *The Spectacle of U.S. Senate Campaigns.*
7. Edie N. Goldenberg and Michael W. Traugott, *Campaigning for Congress* (Washington D.C.: Congressional Quarterly Press, 1984).
8. Kim F. Kahn and Patrick J. Kenney, *The Spectacle of U.S. Senate Campaigns*; Mark C. Westlye, *Senate Elections and Campaign Intensity* (Baltimore, MD: Johns Hopkins Press, 1991).
9. Richard F. Fenno, *Senators on the Campaign Trail* (Norman, OK: University of Oklahoma Press, 1996).
10. Kim F. Kahn, *The Political Consequences of Being a Woman: How Stereotypes Influence the Content and Impact of Statewide Campaigns* (New York, NY: Columbia University Press, 1996).
11. In the analysis in this section, we combine incumbents and winners in open races. We also combine challengers with losers in open races. All articles received one of three scores: –1 negative tone; 0 neutral tone; +1 positive tone. The average tone of articles about incumbents/winners in open races was .01; and the average tone of articles for challengers/losers in open races was –.10. Headlines were also scored as –1 negative tone, 0 neutral tone, and +1 positive tone. The average tone for headlines for incumbents/winners in open race headlines was –.01, and the average tone of headlines for challengers/open race losers was –.05. The average number of criticisms written about incumbents/open winners was 53.68, and 31.81 for challengers/open losers. The average number of negative traits written about incumbents/open winners was 20.18, and 11.01 for challengers/open losers. The average horserace tone was 4.04 for incumbents/open winners, and 2.03 (standard deviation = .63) for challengers/open losers. The horse-race scale ranges from 0 to 4.
12. See Appendix A for information about the measurement of variables.
13. In the OLS models explaining the *amount* of negative coverage (number of criticisms, number of negative traits), we include variables that influence the amount of coverage given to a senate race. In particular, we control for the size of the newspaper, the presence of a governor's race, and the presence of a presidential campaign.
14. We rely on the coefficients in the OLS equation in Table 3.1 to estimate how criticisms vary with the competitiveness of the race. In making these estimates, we hold all remaining variables in the model at their means.
15. See Appendix A for details about how these variables are measured.
16. Michael Basil, Caroline Schooler, and Byron Reeves, "Positive and Negative Political Advertising: Effectiveness of Ads and Perceptions of Candidates," in *Television and Political Advertising*, vol 1: Psychological Processes, ed. Frank Biocca (Hillsdale, NJ: Lawrence Erlbaum Associates, 1991); Kim F. Kahn and John G. Geer, "Creating Impressions: An Experimental Investigation of the Effectiveness of Television Advertising," *Political Behavior* 16 (1994): 93–115.

17. Competitive races are races in which the candidates are separated by less than ten points in preelection polls, while noncompetitive races are contests where the candidates are separated by more than ten points in preelection polls.
18. Large newspapers are newspapers with a newshole greater than 3,000 column inches, while small newspapers are newspapers with newsholes that are 3,000 column inches or smaller. For example, the *Idaho Statesman*, with a newshole of 2,900 column inches was categorized as a small newspaper, while the *Chicago Tribune*, with a newshole of 4,900 column inches was categorized as a large newspaper.
19. Darrell M. West, *Air Wars: Television Campaigning in Election Campaigns, 1952–1992* (Washington D.C.: Congressional Quarterly Press, 1993).
20. The dependent variable in the analysis is the average press assessment of the accuracy of the candidates' advertisements per race. Ad watches were coded as follows: 1 = inaccurate, 2 = mixed accurate and inaccurate, 3 = accurate. For the sample of races, the ad watch variable ranges from 0 to .43 and has a mean of .05 and a standard deviation of .09 for incumbents and a mean of .04 and a standard deviation of .07 for challengers. In the incumbent model, we include incumbents and candidates who win open races. In the challenger model, we include challengers and candidates who lose open races.
21. This is the measure of negativity introduced earlier in the chapter.
22. See Appendix A for how the variables in Table 3.2 are measured. In an earlier analysis predicting assessments of ad watches, we included the gender of the candidate, the quality of the challenger, the seniority of the senator, and the amount of campaign spending, but none of these variables reached statistical significance. Therefore, they were not included in the models presented in Table 3.2.

4

Do Negative Campaigns Inform Citizens?

The mid-1970s were dizzying times in Washington, D.C. In August of 1974 President Richard Nixon resigned, the only American president in history to step down. In the fall of 1976, President Ford, Nixon's vice-president who became president in the wake of Nixon's resignation, was defeated by a one-term governor from Georgia, Jimmy Carter. The Republicans were on the run. The Democrats amassed a 149-seat lead in the House of Representatives after the 1976 elections. And in the Senate, the Democrats led by 24 seats. There were 62 Democratic senators after the 1976 elections. Two freshman Democratic senators who won in 1976 were Daniel Patrick Moynihan from New York and Howard Metzenbaum from Ohio. Senators Moynihan and Metzenbaum would have long careers in the Senate, serving 24 and 18 years respectively. They had many things in common, not the least of which was their political philosophy. Moynihan and Metzenbaum were political liberals. Interest groups that monitor the votes of U.S. senators routinely scored these two senators among the most liberal in the Senate.

Moynihan's liberal views never appeared to alter his chances of winning an election. He captured, on average, 60 percent of the vote in his four senatorial campaigns. The same was not true for Metzenbaum. His liberal tendencies were a point of contention and a potential vulnerability in his three electoral victories. In every election, Metzenbaum campaigned vigorously to defend his liberal views and votes.

Moynihan and Metzenbaum prepared for their third senatorial elections in the summer and autumn of 1988. Moynihan, as usual, coasted to victory, defeating Robert McMillan by thirty-six points. In New York, where competitive campaigns cost millions of dollars, McMillan spent a mere $528,989. Moynihan spent nearly $5 million. McMillan ran no ads explaining that Moynihan was one of the most liberal senators in the Senate. In fact, he spent his meager resources stressing he would reduce crime and encourage "family values."

Metzenbaum was in a different race altogether. His opponent was George Voinovich, the mayor of Cleveland. He was experienced, articulate, and well financed. He spent over $8 million to defeat Metzenbaum, only a few thousand dollars short of what Metzenbaum spent. It was clear from the beginning of the campaign that a key component of Voinovich's strategy was to attack. Specifically, Voinovich attacked Metzenbaum's liberal ideology. Voinovich repeated the phrase, "Metzenbaum is out-of-step with Ohioans, he is too liberal for Ohio," at every opportunity.

Voinovich's attacks were successful at capturing the attention of voters across Ohio, while McMillan's campaign was invisible to most New Yorkers. Voters in Ohio were more aware of the senatorial campaign and more knowledgeable about the candidates than were New Yorkers. In New York, only 30 percent of the people reported exposure to the senate campaign on TV, on radio, or via the newspaper.[1] In Ohio, in contrast, 51 percent of potential voters remember seeing Metzenbaum on TV, remember hearing about Metzenbaum on the radio, and remember reading about him in the paper. Also in Ohio, 95 percent of the citizens surveyed were willing to evaluate Metzenbaum; in New York, only 81 percent of the potential voters were willing to evaluate Moynihan.

Maybe most interesting, Ohioans were much more likely to hold relatively sophisticated views about Metzenbaum compared to what New Yorkers knew about Moynihan. For example, the citizens of Ohio, for the most part, knew Metzenbaum was a liberal. In contrast, the electorate of New York, by and large, seemed unaware of Moynihan's liberal views. Survey respondents in both states were asked by researchers to place Metzenbaum and Moynihan on a seven-point ideological scale, where the respective ends of the scale were labeled "extremely liberal" and "extremely conservative." In New York, only 23 percent of respondents rated Moynihan as a liberal. And, surprisingly, not one respondent thought he was extremely liberal. In contrast, in Ohio, 44 percent thought Metzenbaum was a liberal, and one-fifth of respondents thought he was extremely liberal. Remember, in the late 1980s, Metzenbaum and Moynihan would often receive identical scores from interest groups monitoring their votes in the U.S. Senate. Both senators were quintessential liberals.

What explains the differences in citizens' awareness and knowledge in Ohio and New York? Holding aside, at least for the moment, that the citizens of Ohio are more politically astute than the residents of New York, the answer may lie in the characteristics of the two campaigns. Indeed, there is a great deal of evidence that intense campaigns, characterized by competitive polls, active candidates, and an interested media, increase citizens' awareness and knowledge of the competing candidates.[2] Unquestionably, Metzenbaum's campaign was more intense than Moynihan's. Metzenbaum maintained a lead in the polls, but the polls always indicated that the race was competitive. Moynihan, in contrast, led by as many as fifty points in early October. Metzenbaum and Voinovich spent over $16 million, whereas Moynihan and McMillan spent less than $6 million. The differences in spending are dramatic. Metzenbaum and Voinovich spent $1.54 per potential voter in Ohio, while Moynihan and McMillan spent only .27 cents per voter in New York. The Cleveland *Plain Dealer*, the largest circulating paper in Ohio, produced dozens of articles about the race. The New York *Daily News*, the largest circulating paper in New York, published a total of seventeen articles during the entire race.

There is little doubt that intense campaigns provide the motivation and requisite information for citizens to become informed about competing candidates. Yet, is there something beyond the sheer intensity of campaigns that influences voters' awareness of and information about candidates? What about the tone of the information presented during campaigns? Does positive or negative information affect citizens equally? As an example, would Ohioans have gleaned as much about Metzenbaum's liberal views if Voinovich focused on his own record instead of offering sharp criticisms that Metzenbaum was "too liberal to represent Ohio?" In this chapter we are interested in examining whether the tone of campaign messages affects citizens' levels of information about candidates.

THE EFFECTS OF NEGATIVE INFORMATION ON CITIZENS

There are two questions, at least, that come to the fore when thinking about how negative information influences what citizens know about competing candidates. First, do negative messages affect citizens' levels of knowledge about the competing candidates more dramatically than positive messages? And, second, do different types of negative messages have differing effects on voters' levels of information?

As for the first question, it is possible, even likely, that negative information influences voters' awareness of campaigns and knowledge about the competing candidates more dramatically than positive information. There is a widespread belief among social psychologists that negative information attracts people's attention more readily than positive information and negative information has a stronger influence on people's attitudes than positive information.[3]

People attend to negative stimuli and events in their environments much more quickly than they do to positive information. This is true even if the amount of positive information is far greater than the amount of negative information, and even when individuals are distracted by the swirl of events associated with daily life.[4]

The reasoning for the immediate attention to negative information is that, more times than not, it carries with it harbingers of events or situations that people want to avoid. The swift and seamless attention to negative information is referred to by social psychologists as "automatic vigilance."[5] To be sure, there is plenty of negative and critical information in contemporary campaigns. And, sure enough, researchers have demonstrated that people tend to remember more information from negative commercials than from positive ads.[6]

People not only attend to negative information more vigilantly than positive information, negative information has a greater influence on their evaluations and assessments than positive information. Negative information has a greater impact because negative messages carry information about potentially dangerous or costly outcomes. Researchers from fields as diverse as decision making, impression formation, and communication have shown that people strive to avoid behaviors and situations that increase the risks of undesirable outcomes.[7] Thus, people weigh information about the likelihood of losses more heavily than information about the probability of gains. Consistent with the notion of automatic vigilance, people "automatically evaluate" events that may negatively affect their lives.[8] Judgments based on negative information are made quickly, almost effortlessly.

Negative messages consistently identify risks more sharply than equivalent positive information. This is especially true in political campaigns. Candidates intentionally identify, discuss, and debate the risks associated with electing their opponents (e.g., my opponent will raise taxes, my opponent wants to socialize medicine, my opponent wants to change Social Security, my opponent will send U.S. kids to war). Messages that articulate risks associated with certain electoral outcomes may be especially influential.[9] In contrast, strictly positive messages are devoid of any discussions of risks. When candidates discuss the positive aspects of their candidacies, they focus on their personal qualities or issue positions with absolutely no mention of risk assessments.

The 2000 senatorial campaign in Washington between Maria Cantwell and Slade Gorton illustrates how negative rather than positive messages left an impression on the citizens of Washington. Republican Senator Gorton was seeking his fourth term as senator. Cantwell, a former Democratic member of the House, defeated in 1994, returned to politics to capture a U.S. Senate seat. This was an intense race from the beginning. Cantwell spent over $11 million and Gorton spent over $6 million to spread their messages. The polls indicated that Gorton had a slim lead in September but by early October the race was "too close to call." It remained competitive to the end. The press across the state of Washington followed the race intently.

The candidates criticized one another on a range of issues. They squabbled in the press, via ads, in speeches, and in debates. They disagreed on campaign finance reform, on prescription drugs, on Social Security, on abortion, on foreign affairs, on gun control, and maybe most dramatically, on the environment. The environmental issue centered on a gold mine proposed for the rural Washington county of Okanogan. The issue generated the classic split between environmentalists and industry. Environmentalists opposed the mine because the cyanide-leaching process used to extract the gold might seep into underground drinking water. The Texas company that wanted to mine the land, Battle Mountain Gold, claimed the process was safe. Gorton favored the mine and authored legislation in Congress to enable the mine to move forward. Cantwell opposed, vigorously.

Their disagreements played out in ads and in several debates. On October 30, 2000, both candidates appeared in a televised debate. The issue of the mine surfaced quickly. Cantwell criticized Gorton for his close cooperation with Battle Mountain Gold. She charged, "Senator, you were a world-class promoter of that mine. You wrote, on your knees, language for the lobbyists." Gorton responded, "She ignores 80 percent of the county who want economic development." To stress the environmentalists' position that cyanide-leaching may seep into drinking water, Cantwell produced an advertisement that began with a picturesque setting of the mountains. Then, a black cloud covered the screen and the commercial moved to a young girl drinking water from a faucet, clearly suggesting that the mine may poison the water, endangering the health of children. In addition, the Sierra Club attacked Gorton with radio and TV ads for several months, criticizing him for a series of "anti-environmental" votes, beyond the issue of the mine.

The testy exchanges were not lost on the citizens of Washington. CNN exit polls asked voters which was more important to them, the health of the environment or economic growth. Fifty percent of the 1,743 respondents said the environment. Among these respondents, 69 percent reported voting for Cantwell. Forty percent of respondents said they supported economic growth. A whopping 74 percent of these folks voted for Gorton. These data suggest that voters cast ballots for the candidate that most closely supported their beliefs on the vexing balance of economic growth and environmental protection. It is quite possible that the negative attacks by the candidates allowed voters to make the connection between their beliefs regarding the trade-off between the environment and the economy and their views of the candidates.

In contrast, the candidates ran several exclusively positive messages, but they did not capture the attention of voters. For example, mixed among the candidates' issue messages, Cantwell and Gordon stressed several personal qualities. Cantwell emphasized that she was the first in her family to earn a college degree. In fact, one of her ads stressed that her father was a concrete worker and her mother was a secretary, yet Maria achieved a college education. Gorton, for good reason, never attacked her working-class upbringing or her hard-earned college education. Gorton, on the other hand, emphasized his experience in the Senate. He stressed his influence on committees and his understanding of how legislation is crafted and brought to the president's desk for final signature. He emphasized his ability to bring projects and federal dollars to Washington. Cantwell's only response to Gorton's positive self-promotion was the nebulous phrase, "it is time for a change."

The positive promotion of their personal qualities did not capture citizens' attention to the same degree as the contentious discussion over issues. Again, CNN researchers asked voters to identify which was more important to them during the campaign, issues or qualities. Overwhelmingly, the voters of Washington said issues. Sixty percent of voters responded that issues were most important, compared to 35 percent who responded personal qualities.

Not All Negative Messages Are the Same

The senatorial campaign in Washington illustrates the central point that negative and critical comparative campaign messages may resonate with voters more dramatically than positive messages. However, voters may view certain negative messages as more useful than others. Voters may find some negative messages, known in contemporary American politics as "mudslinging," at best unhelpful and at worst offensive. Voters are looking for information that addresses relevant topics and is presented in an appropriate manner. In contrast, information unrelated to governing and presented in a shrill and harsh manner is of little use to voters.[10]

An overriding characteristic of mudslinging is its negative content, filled with criticisms and negative assessments. This negative content is likely to catch the attention of voters. If this is the case, citizens may be more aware of information about candidates in races filled with mudslinging. However, if the content of the messages is irrelevant to their lives, then people may not use the information when forming candidate evaluations. Put simply, individuals evaluate information that bears some relevance to their lives. People effortlessly sort information according to how germane it is to their health and well-being. If the connections between negative information and people's lives are trivial and insignificant, then citizens have virtually no incentive to evaluate the information.

Negative political messages are useful when they discuss topics related directly to governing.[11] If candidates are incumbent senators or have served in other public offices, then criticisms of past performance can help voters assess candidates' performance. Critiques may be aimed at a series of topics such as candidates' voting records and public statements, candidates' reactions to political events, and candidates' attendance in Congress. In addition, information that may provide clues about a candidate's direction for the future may guide citizens' evaluations. Thus, criticisms of contemporary issue positions, critiques of plans to address local or national problems, and assessments of goals for government are useful pieces of information. In the case of challengers or candidates for open seats, topics such as previous work experience, current issue positions, and general political beliefs are relevant for debate and commentary. All of these subjects are, in one way or another, related to governing;

they provide insight into what candidates have been doing and what they can be expected to do in the future.

In contrast, certain topics seem to be only tangentially related to governing performance, and for this reason may be of little interest to voters. These topics include candidates' behaviors as young people during or shortly after their college years, past marital problems, previous financial complications, as well as old business dealings. In addition, issue positions held in the distant past may seem unconnected to contemporary concerns. Voters appear to understand that politicians' policy positions sometimes evolve and change. They are most interested in current positions and beliefs. These examples highlight attitudes and actions that have little predictive power or educative value for understanding candidates' current political actions and attitudes.

Beyond the usefulness of the information, voters are also sensitive to the tone in which the critical information is presented. Citizens are less interested in campaigns when the negative information is produced in a shrill manner. On balance, most people do not listen to or absorb harsh public statements. When candidates' voices are strident and the commentary is vicious, citizens turn away. In the parlance of contemporary high-tech America, when voters come in contact with harsh ads they "flip channels" or "mute the sound." Since politics is not a daily priority for most Americans, there is little incentive for citizens to listen to discordant political discourse. There is little reason to expect people to subject themselves intentionally to nasty exchanges by politicians when their principal interests lie elsewhere.

The 2000 senatorial campaign in Minnesota between Republican incumbent Rod Grams and Democratic challenger Mark Dayton was characterized by a good deal of mudslinging.[12] The candidates delivered strident messages on largely irrelevant topics repeatedly during the campaign. Although Dayton maintained a lead in the polls throughout October, the race was competitive. Dayton spent over $11 million, mostly from his own family fortune, and Grams spent over $6 million. This was an intense campaign from start to finish.

There was a good deal of discussion on several issues, such as gun control, the environment, health care generally, prescription drugs, Social Security, taxes, and education. Grams and Dayton disagreed with one another on all key issues. Their disagreements were the subjects of many TV and radio ads. The candidates clashed in several debates, and the major newspapers spent a great deal of time discussing the candidates' issue positions. In many respects, the detailed and critical commentary of policy matters in the Minnesota race was similar to the discussions taking place in the senatorial race in Washington between Gorton and Cantwell. But in Minnesota, the discussions went past disagreements on the issues and turned into mudslinging, not true in the campaign in the state of Washington.

Grams and Dayton not only discussed topics that were only tangentially relevant to governing, but their presentations of information were often harsh and their interactions with one another were shrill. One contentious and large-ly irrelevant topic concerned Dayton's activities as an antiwar protester in the late 1960s and early 1970s. Dayton graduated from Yale in 1969. Student protests against the Vietnam War were in full bloom by 1969 and continued until the end of the war in 1973. Dayton was an active antiwar protester. His activities, along with many other war protesters, were monitored by the FBI as well as by staff in the Nixon White House.

Grams sought to make Dayton's antiwar activities a campaign issue. By the fall of 2000, the Vietnam War had been over for twenty-seven years and Dayton's activities were nearly thirty years old. Dayton was in his early twen-ties at the time of his protests. The war itself was extremely controversial and, by the early 1970s evoked considerable criticism from an array of American citizens. In the end, Dayton's activities between 1969 and 1973 provided lit-tle useful information about how he might handle the issues facing Minnesota and the nation in the first decade of a new century. The negative message pre-sented by Grams about Dayton's antiwar activities was only tangentially rel-evant for the 2000 campaign.

A more relevant topic discussed by the candidates was the cost of pre-scription drugs. The issue was timely, as the cost of prescription drugs had es-calated dramatically in the 1990s. In addition, the issue was being discussed by the presidential candidates, George W. Bush and Al Gore. However, Grams and Dayton's campaign rhetoric was harsh. Dayton argued that the price of nearly all prescription drugs should be lowered and he spent considerable time criticizing the profiteering of large pharmaceutical companies, often re-ferring to large drug manufacturers as "profiteering drug lords." During the campaign, it was discovered that Dayton held stock in two drug companies. Upon this discovery, he immediately sold the stock. Grams and the Republi-cans pounced immediately on the appearance of hypocrisy. Their criticisms were strident. Their language was hyperbolic. A Republican Party mailer sent out across the state began, "Meet Minnesota's No. 1 Drug Lord," featuring a black-and-white picture of Dayton. Dayton responded that the mailer was "beyond irresponsible." The two sparred about the "drug lord" language in several TV and radio debates and in ads.

A final example captures the level of mudslinging in the Minnesota race. In late October, Grams used his mother to deliver a negative message. In a commercial that ran statewide, Audrey Grams sitting in her kitchen calmly ad-dressed the citizens of Minnesota.

Have you ever had someone spend a million dollars a week telling lies about someone you love? I've seen those Mark Dayton ads. He should be ashamed. They're just crazy. He's lying about Rod, and trying to pull the wool over our eyes. Rod cut taxes, and he's the one who did the lockbox to save Social Se-curity. He's got a good prescription drug plan, too. You can trust Rod. I should know. I raised him. Mark Dayton? Uff-da. Vote for Rod.

To be sure, candidates' mothers have campaigned for their children in the past. The most notable example may be Rose Fitzgerald Kennedy, who spent many hours campaigning for John Kennedy in his initial run for the U.S. Congress in 1946. On the campaign trail, she refused to deliver a political campaign speech on the grounds that followers were not interested in her politics. Rather, she talked about her family and spun stories about her years as an ambassador's wife at the Court of St. James in England.[13] Her style stands in direct contrast to the confrontational approach used by Grams's mother, who unabashedly called Dayton a liar.

In the end, the Minnesota race was replete with discussions of topics that were only marginally related to governing and with language that offends common courtesy and propriety.[14] The good people of Minnesota knew the race had "crossed the line." A staggering 88 percent of respondents to CNN exit polls noted that one or both candidates had attacked unfairly. Fifty-seven percent said Dayton attacked unfairly; 63 percent thought Grams attacked unfairly. In fact, 42 percent believed that both candidates had behaved badly.

The cases of Washington and Minnesota in 2000 illustrate that citizens appear to exhibit more heightened awareness of candidates and campaigns as the rate of negative information increases relative to positive information. And, maybe more striking, citizens seem to assess more accurately the content of campaign discussion as negative information increases in their environment. Finally, these cases bring to light the possibility that citizens are fully capable of understanding that certain types of negative messages, those irrelevant to governing and those harsh in tone, are of little value when assessing rival candidates. The campaigns between Gorton and Cantwell and Grams and Dayton prompt us to examine more systematically the relationship between negative campaign messages and voters' awareness and understanding of the campaign. We move to expand our analyses beyond illustrative examples to nearly 100 senatorial campaigns.

THE RELATIONSHIP BETWEEN NEGATIVE INFORMATION AND CITIZENS' ATTITUDES

To be sure, there is a long history of research examining the impact of campaigns on voters' understanding of politics.[15] Recently, scholars have begun to examine the specific impact of negative messages on voters' views of candidates and campaigns. The findings from these research efforts are unsettled, even contradictory. For example, on the question of whether negative campaign information "sours citizens on politics," there is conflicting evidence. One review of existing studies found that fifteen scholarly reports demonstrated that negative advertisements turned people off to politics, while fourteen studies found that attack advertising had a positive effect on people's view of politics.[16] In addition, research studies fail to yield consistent findings on whether negative advertisements create positive or negative affects for the candidate (sponsor) or opponent (target) of the ad. There is some evidence that negative ads help sponsors, while other studies reveal that negative ads hurt sponsors, with a third set of data suggesting negative commercials have no effect on voters.[17]

We think some of the confusion generated by contemporary research is due, to some extent, to the methodologies employed in these studies. For example, some previous studies have relied on experimental designs where citizens are shown positive or negative ads in a laboratory. There have been very few efforts to examine voters in their work or home environments. Also, the vast majority of prior studies have focused exclusively on the negative messages emanating from the candidates' campaigns, with little or no attention given to the tone of the news media's message. Furthermore, most of the studies looking at the impact of negative campaigning have failed to distinguish between legitimate criticisms of the candidates and "mudslinging." Finally, few studies have examined the impact of negative campaigning on voters' understanding of candidates and campaigns.[18]

In this chapter, we hope to avoid some of the problems associated with earlier research and to increase our understanding of the role of negative information in campaigns. We look specifically at how the variation in the tone of candidates' campaigns and the variance in the tone of the news media's messages influence what citizens know about the candidates.

In order to isolate the impact of negative messages on voters, it is necessary to consider rival factors that may also influence voters' understanding of senate campaigns. To begin with, the campaign context affects what people know about political candidates.[19] For example, as the competitiveness of campaigns increases, people become more knowledgeable about campaigns and candidates.[20] Similarly, as the candidates spend more money disseminating their messages, citizens are more likely to learn the candidates' campaign themes. In addition, the status of the candidate may influence learning among citizens. Races between an incumbent senator and a challenger tend to generate more interest and attention compared to open races. Therefore, knowledge about the candidates may be greater in races with incumbents.

The characteristics of the candidates may also influence people's understanding of the political contestants. People are likely to know more about senior senators as well as experienced and skilled challengers. Such candidates have been part of the political landscape longer and citizens are more familiar with these figures. Similarly, the gender of the candidates may affect what people know about the Senate contestants. Women seeking high elective office remain rare and we know that people are likely to remember information that is unique or surprising.[21] Therefore, voters unaccustomed to seeing women compete for the U.S. Senate will be more likely to take notice when the campaign is something other than the typical male versus male contest.

Finally, the habits, preferences, and skills of citizens also influence their knowledge about campaigns. Just as no two campaigns are alike, no two voters are alike. People differ dramatically in their levels of political sophistication about politics.[22] Some citizens have an extensive understanding of politics and a great deal of stored information about policies and political candidates. Others know very little about political affairs. People's levels of political expertise are likely to affect what they know about the contestants in specific senatorial campaigns.

Similarly, citizens who rely heavily on the news media are likely to have more information about the competing Senate candidates.[23] In addition, people who are more interested in politics will know more about specific Senate elections[24] Formal education also influences attention to and involvement in elections since schooling increases an individual's ability to acquire information about all topics, including campaigns.[25] Voters also vary in the strengths of their attachments to political parties, with strong partisans routinely acquiring news about political events.[26] Therefore, the partisan profiles of citizens are likely to influence voters' understanding of the candidates.

THE IMPACT OF NEGATIVITY ON AWARENESS OF THE CANDIDATES

To examine how the tone of the campaign influences people's understanding of senate campaigns, we develop three complementary measures of negativity. First, we create a measure of negativity to assess the proportion of negative to positive advertisements aired by each candidate in the campaigns.[27] Second, to measure the negative coverage in the press, we develop a measure where the number of critical paragraphs written about each candidate is divided by the total number of paragraphs published about the candidate.[28] Finally, we create a measure to assess the amount of "mudslinging" during the campaign since it is important to distinguish between legitimate critical information presented by the candidates and the news media, on the one hand, and negative attacks presented in a harsh manner on inappropriate topics, on the other hand.[29] We relied on responses to the campaign manager survey to identify "mudslinging" campaigns.[30]

EXPOSURE TO THE CANDIDATES

Candidates strive to get their messages across to potential supporters. Candidates with resources spend enormous sums of money running political advertisements. In addition, candidates try to generate "free" media exposure via newspapers, television news, and radio. Does the tone of the campaign influence people's reported exposure to the candidates? For instance, are citizens more likely to remember seeing a candidate on the television if the candidate was the subject of an attack advertisement? Similarly, are voters more likely to remember reading about candidates in newspapers if the information in the press was negative?

To measure citizens' exposure to the candidates, we look at whether respondents in the NES Senate Election Study reported seeing the candidates on television, remembered reading about the candidates in the newspaper, or recalled hearing about the candidates on the radio.[31] Certain types of negativity do, indeed, influence exposure to the candidates. First, mudslinging heightens voters' exposure to the incumbent, but not for challengers (See Table 4.1 on page 76). As the rhetoric of the campaign degenerates, becoming less civil and focusing on topics with little relevance to governing, citizens are more likely to report being exposed to the sitting senators. Voters undoubtedly are taken aback by some of the more nasty commercials and discussions. Thus, for the reasons discussed earlier, they are more likely to take notice of the campaign.

Second, the proportion of criticisms in the press does not increase people's likelihood of reporting exposure to the candidates. The pattern is consistent. As criticisms increase for incumbents and challengers relative to the total amount of news about the campaign, reported exposure to the candidates does not increase.

Turning to the impact of the candidates' ads, incumbents who run negative advertisements increase exposure for challengers, but decrease exposure for their own candidacies. Why? Typically, negative ads developed by incumbents spend the entire 30 seconds criticizing the challenger with absolutely no mention of the senator. In fact, 61 percent of the negative advertisement produced by incumbents are purely negative, with no reference to the incumbent senator. For example, Senator Lincoln Chafee ran an advertisement criticizing his opponent, Bob Weygand, that focused squarely on Weygand:

> Bob Weygand's campaign is an insult to voters. He is unable to face the truth. Now he's been caught embroidering the truth about prescription drugs. His government price control plan cuts prices for drug vendors, not seniors. Cancer organizations oppose it. The Veteran's Administration says Weygand's plan may raise drug costs by millions. . . .

It is easy to see why Chafee's advertisement, by talking exclusively about Weygand's candidacy, did not increase reported exposure for Chafee. Chafee failed to mention his own name in the ad, yet he mentioned Weygand's name twice.

In contrast, negative advertisements sponsored by challengers increase exposure for their own candidacies. This may be the case because challengers begin campaigns as virtual unknowns. Therefore, *any* campaign activity increases voters' awareness of these candidates.[32]

Turning to the remaining explanations for citizens' exposure to the candidates, the characteristics of the candidates influence exposure levels. For instance, people report greater exposure to senior senators, compared to more

TABLE 4.1   THE INFLUENCE OF NEGATIVE INFORMATION
ON VOTERS' EXPOSURE TO CANDIDATES

	EXPOSURE TO INCUMBENTS		EXPOSURE TO CHALLENGERS	
Proportion of Negative Information				
Incumbents' Ads Negative	−.11 (.04)**	−.02	.11 (.06)*	.02
Challengers' Ads Negative	−.003 (.03)	−.01	.11 (.04)**	.03
Press Criticisms of Incumbent	−.08 (.15)	−.01		
Press Criticisms of Challenger			−.10 (17)	−.01
Mudslinging	.02 (.01)*	.01	.02 (.02)	.01
Characteristics of the Race				
Candidate Spending	.03 (.006)**	.04	.09 (.007)**	.13
Competition	.002 (.0007)**	.03	.01 (.0009)**	.19
Open	2.20 (.03)**	.72	1.93 (.03)**	.59
Characteristics of Candidates				
Seniority	.007 (.001)**	.05		
Challenger Quality			.01 (.002)**	.06
Gender	.24 (.06)**	.03	.06 (.03)*	.02
Characteristics of Citizens				
Party Attachment	.02 (.009)	.01	.0008 (.01)	.01
Education	.004 (.003)	.01	.008 (.004)*	.02
Attention to the News	.04 (.002)**	.14	.04 (.003)**	.13
Sophistication	.07 (.006)**	.10	.08 (.008)**	.10
Interest	.03 (.007)**	.04	.05 (.009)**	.06
Constant	−.76 (.07)**		−2.06 (.09)**	
N	6110		6110	
R^2	.62		.44	

The dependent variable in both models is voters' exposure to the candidates on TV, on radio, and in the newspaper. In each cell, we present the OLS unstandardized coefficient followed by the standard error in parentheses, and the standardized coefficient.

All p-values are two-tailed.

**p < .01

*p < .05

junior colleagues. People are also more likely to report exposure to quality challengers, compared to challengers with less skill and little prior political experience. The gender of the candidate also makes a difference, with people reporting greater exposure to female incumbents and female challengers, compared to male counterparts. Female candidates, because they are still relatively rare in politics, "stand out," making them more likely to be noticed and remembered, especially compared to male candidates.

The context of the race is also important, with campaign spending and competition significantly increasing exposure for both incumbents and challengers. Finally, the characteristics of the citizens dramatically influence self-reported exposure to the candidates. For instance, respondents who are politically sophisticated, who are interested in politics, and who pay attention to the media report higher exposure to challengers and incumbents than other respondents.

WILLINGNESS TO EVALUATE THE CANDIDATES

Before voters support a candidate, they need to become familiar with the candidate beyond mere exposure to the candidate on TV, on radio, or in the newspaper. During campaigns, candidates seek to increase voters' knowledge of their candidacies.[33] We measure familiarity by looking at whether citizens are willing to evaluate a candidate. In particular, survey respondents are asked whether they are willing to rate the senate candidate on a "feeling thermometer" ranging from 0 to 100.[34] If respondents indicate a willingness to rate the candidate (i.e., respondents rated the candidates somewhere from 0 to 100), they are coded 1. The remaining respondents are scored 0. As one would expect, respondents are more willing to evaluate incumbents than challengers. In particular, we find that 91 percent of the respondents rate sitting senators, while only 71 percent rate the challengers.

Does the negativity of the race influence people's willingness to rate the candidates? To answer this question, we employ the same measures of negativity used in the prior analysis. The findings for willingness to rate candidates parallel the earlier findings for exposure (see Table 4.2 on page 78). Mudslinging, because it is at best abrasive and at worst offensive, catches the attention of voters. As mudslinging increases, willingness to rate the incumbents increases significantly, and the probability of evaluating challengers increases modestly, but not significantly. This finding suggests that campaigns filled with mudslinging are hard to miss. Controversial speeches and advertisements bring attention to candidates and increase people's willingness to evaluate politicians.

As for the press, also consistent with exposure, there appears to be no relationship between the measures of media criticisms and citizens' willingness to rate the incumbents or challengers. The press criticisms do not encourage voters to evaluate the competing candidates.

Turning to the candidates' ads, the tone of the incumbents' advertisements has a consistent and powerful impact on citizens' willingness to rate the challengers. As discussed earlier, incumbents' negative ads focus on challengers, thereby enhancing voters' awareness of challengers. For example, a negative advertisement aired by Democratic Senator Chuck Robb in Virginia may have increased familiarity with his opponent, Republican George Allen. In the advertisement, the narrator explains that Robb "signed the landmark Chesapeake Bay agreement" as governor, then "supported the Clean Air and

TABLE 4.2   HOW NEGATIVE INFORMATION
INFLUENCES VOTERS' WILLINGNESS TO RATE THE CANDIDATES

	WILLING TO RATE INCUMBENT		WILLING TO RATE CHALLENGER	
Proportion of Negative Information				
Incumbents' Ads Negative	−.12 (.11)	−.01	.48 (.09)**	.27
Challengers' Ads Negative	−.12 (.08)	−.14	.05 (.05)	.04
Press Criticisms of Incumbent	−.47 (.40)	−.10		
Press Criticisms of Challenger			−.17 (.22)	−.03
Mudslinging	.11 (.04)**	.26	.002 (.03)	.01
Characteristics of the Race				
Candidate Spending	.02 (.02)	.13	.15 (.01)**	.58
Competition	.005 (.002)**	.37	.01 (.001)**	.44
Open	.01 (.08)	.01	−.10 (05)*	−.08
Characteristics of Candidates				
Seniority	.01 (.004)**	.29		
Challenger Quality			.01 (.003)**	.15
Gender	.77 (.30)**	.38	.08 (.04)*	.07
Characteristics of Citizens				
Party Attachment	.05 (.02)*	.18	.03 (.02)	.07
Education	.04 (.007)**	.45	.02 (.005)**	.14
Attention to the News	.03 (.006)**	.17	.08 (.04)*	.73
Sophistication	.29 (.02)**	1.68	.14 (.01)**	.49
Interest	.07 (.02)**	.36	.05 (.01)**	.16
Constant	−.68 (.19)**		−1.90 (.13)**	
N	6110		6110	
Percent Correctly Predicted	92%		76%	

The dependent variable in both models is voters' willingness to rate the candidates.

In each cell, we present the unstandardized logit coefficient, followed by the standard error in parentheses, followed by the standardized coefficient.

All p-values are two-tailed.

***p < .01

**p < .05

*p < .10

Clean Water Act and fought to protect Virginia from out-of-state trash" in the Senate. Allen, the ad says, "sued to overturn the Clean Air Act, refused to enforce environmental laws," and "stood by while a campaign contributor polluted a tributary of the Chesapeake." The ad cites the League of Conservation

Voters' rating of Allen's environmental record as "one of the worst in the nation." This advertisement, by discussing Allen's environmental record, may have increased citizens' willingness to rate Allen.

Finally, as expected, other forces besides negativity increase voters' willingness to evaluate the candidates. For example, the closeness of the race increases people's likelihood of rating the incumbent and the challenger. Certain types of candidates are more likely to be evaluated, such as female senators and quality challengers. Finally, the characteristics of respondents also influence willingness to rate the candidates, with politically sophisticated, educated, interested, and media-savvy citizens being more likely to evaluate incumbents and challengers.

THE RELATIONSHIP BETWEEN NEGATIVITY AND CAMPAIGN THEMES

Moving beyond simple exposure and a willingness to rate the candidates, it is important to see if negative messages influence people's understanding of campaign themes. It is one thing to demonstrate that negative messages increase familiarity with the candidates, but it is quite another to discover that negative messages improve citizens' understanding of what candidates are talking about. Candidates fret constantly about whether their messages are received and understood by potential voters.[35] More broadly still, proponents of democratic elections make certain assumptions about campaigns. For example, an important element of campaigns is that candidates discuss and debate the most important issues of the day and citizens use these discussions when evaluating the competing candidates. Does the tone of the campaign influence citizens' awareness and understanding of the candidates' campaign themes?

We begin by examining whether voters are able to detect when candidates make negative messages the primary focus of their campaigns. Do voters recognize the presence of negative themes if candidates spend a substantial amount of time and resources criticizing their opponents? To investigate this question, we look at respondents' answers to the following NES/SES question: "In your state, what issue did the candidates talk about the most during the campaign for the Senate?" We look at whether people are more likely to identify a negative issue in races where the messages delivered during the campaign are more negative in tone.[36]

To assess the negativity of the senate contest, we measure the proportion of *both* candidates' ads that were negative in tone and we calculate the proportion of media coverage that included criticisms of *both* incumbents and challengers. The mudslinging variable, because it already captures mudslinging by both candidates, remains unchanged. We continue to control for forces that are related to voters' likelihood of mentioning a negative issue theme, such as the characteristics of the candidates, campaigns, and voters.

Voters are more likely to mention negative themes as campaigns degenerate into mudslinging affairs. And, people are more likely to mention a negative issue theme as the proportion of negative ads increase (see Table 4.3). Taken together, it appears that the negative information delivered by the candidates makes it significantly more likely that voters will cite negativity as the primary issue of the campaign.

TABLE 4.3   THE INFLUENCE OF NEGATIVE INFORMATION
ON VOTERS' KNOWLEDGE OF CANDIDATES' CAMPAIGN THEMES

	IDENTIFICATION OF NEGATIVE THEME		IDENTIFICATION OF CORRECT THEME	
Proportion of Negative Information				
Candidates' Ads	.28 (.12)*	.27	.43 (.08)**	.29
Press Criticisms of Candidates	.57 (.45)	.13	−.42 (.32)	.06
Mudslinging	.04 (.02)*	.16	.07 (.02)**	.20
Characteristics of the Race				
Candidate Spending	−.02 (.01)*	−.13	.02 (.01)*	.09
Competition	.01 (.002)**	.76	.005 (.001)**	.26
Open	.09 (.08)	.12	.32 (06)**	.30
Characteristics of Candidates				
Seniority	−.001 (.004)	−.03	−.03 (.003)**	−.63
Challenger Quality	.004 (.004)	.10	−.02 (.002)**	.36
Gender	.02 (.07)	.03	.24 (.04)**	.24
Characteristics of Citizens				
Party Attachment	−.09 (.02)**	−.34	.01 (.02)	.03
Education	.03 (.01)**	.34	.01 (.006)**	.08
Attention to the News	.01 (.006)**	.16	.01 (.004)**	.11
Sophistication	.11 (.02)**	.66	.06 (.01)**	.25
Interest	−.04 (.02)*	−.22	.06 (.01)**	.22
Constant	−1.91 (.13)**		3.42 (.16)**	
N	6110		6110	
Percent Correctly Predicted	92%		80%	

The dependent variable in the model presented in the first column is the voters' willingness to identify a negative issue as the main theme of the campaign. The dependent variable in the model presented in the second column is the voters' ability to perceive correctly the candidates' main campaign themes.

In each cell, we present the unstandardized logit coefficient, followed by the standard error in parentheses, followed by the standardized coefficient.

All p-values are two-tailed.

**p < .01

*p < .05

Also, the tone of media coverage does not influence voters' awareness of negative campaign themes. That is, voters' likelihood of mentioning negativity as the primary theme of the campaign is unaffected by the proportion of negative to positive media coverage. It appears that voters' awareness of the negativity of the campaign comes from the candidates, not from the news media.

Turning to the characteristics of the race, voters are more likely to identify negative themes when campaign spending increases and when races are more competitive. We also find that sophistication about politics, interest in politics, strength of party attachment, and education level are all related to citizen's awareness of negative campaign themes.

Voters clearly become more aware of negative campaign themes as candidates "go negative." However, are voters more likely to correctly identify the candidates' main themes as negative information increases? To answer this question, we look at whether the amount and type of negative information in the campaign influences the correspondence between the candidates' main campaign themes and citizens' perceptions of these main themes.[37] Naturally, when examining the relationship between negativity and correct identification of the themes of the campaign, we control for forces that may be related to citizens' perceptions of candidates' themes, such as the type of candidates running, the nature of the race, and the characteristics of the citizens.

Voters' knowledge of candidates' main themes improves as mudslinging escalates. In other words, mudslinging increases the likelihood that voters perceive more accurately the main themes stressed by the candidates (see Table 4.3).

In addition, as candidates increase the flow of negative information during a campaign, citizens' perceptions of the main themes of the campaign become more accurate. Voters understand more accurately what candidates are discussing when the airwaves are filled with negative commercials, compared to campaigns with only positive commercials.

To illustrate, Brian Schweitzer of Montana, in his challenge of Senator Conrad Burns, aired a commercial criticizing Burns for voting against minimum wage increases. The advertisement tells voters that while "Montana is dead last in wages," Burns voted "18 times against the minimum wage." Burns also voted to "let corporations deny workers overtime pay" and to "allow corporations to raid retirement funds and cheat workers out of benefits." The ad accused Burns of hypocrisy, noting that he voted "himself a $23,000 raise." This advertisement, by clearly presenting Senator Burns's position on the minimum wage, provides information on the risks associated with reelecting Burns. The advertisement also points out the hypocrisy of Burns's position. Such an advertisement may have enhanced voters' awareness of the main themes of the campaign.

In contrast, the proportion of negative to positive criticisms in the press does not influence voters' levels of knowledge of the candidates' main themes.

That is, the critical content of news coverage does not influence voters' accuracy about the candidates' campaign themes.

Finally, the characteristics of the citizens continue to have a strong impact, significantly influencing voters' ability to name the candidates' main themes. Voters' education level, interest in campaigns, propensity to follow the news, and level of sophistication about politics are all positively correlated with citizens' understanding of the candidates' messages. Also, close contests, races with quality challengers, senior senators, and female candidates encourage more accurate recall of the candidates' messages.

To illustrate the key findings in Table 4.3 (page 80), we convert the statistical coefficients in Table 4.3 to probabilities. This allows us to demonstrate graphically how changes in negative information influence (1) citizens' likelihood of identifying a negative theme, and (2) citizens' likelihood of mentioning the actual themes of the campaign. For example, when advertisements during the campaign are positive and mudslinging is absent, citizens have a .37 probability of identifying a negative campaign theme, holding all rival forces constant (see Figure 4.1).[38] In contrast, there is almost a 50–50 chance (i.e., .48) that voters will identify a negative theme when the commercials are negative in tone and mudslinging is at its peak, *ceteris paribus*.

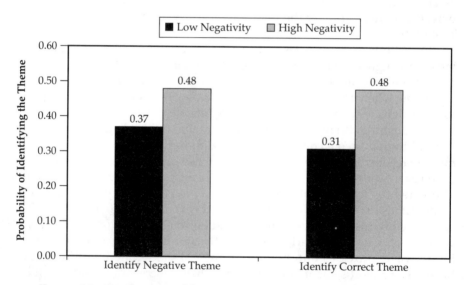

FIGURE 4.1   THE IMPACT OF NEGATIVITY ON KNOWLEDGE OF THE CAMPAIGN

Note: The probabilities are derived from the coefficients in Table 4.3. We vary the tone of the advertisements and the presence of mudslinging, and leave all remaining variables at their means.
Source: The 1988–1992 NES/SES.

The probability of identifying the correct theme of the campaign changes even more dramatically, depending on the tone of the campaign messages. For example, in races where there are no negative ads and no mudslinging, voters have a .31 probability of recalling correctly the candidates' main themes. In contrast, voters have a .48 probability of accurately recalling the candidates' themes in campaigns filled with negative commercials and mudslinging. This amount of change is striking. As campaigns go from completely positive in tone to extremely negative, the probability of citizens identifying correctly the main themes of campaigns climbs from less than one-in-three to nearly one-in-two, holding all rival forces constant.

SUMMARY

This chapter began with a simple question: Are voters more knowledgeable about candidates and campaigns when the rhetoric of the campaign is more negative than positive? The simple answer is yes. As campaigns become nasty, citizens are more likely to learn about candidates, and they become more knowledgeable about the content of campaign messages. The tone of the candidates' advertisements also influences people's awareness of the candidates. Overall, when voters live and work in states with more negativity, they are more likely to recall being exposed to the candidates; they are more likely to evaluate the candidates; they are more likely to recognize the main campaign messages.

The source of the negative messages delivered during campaigns matters. Negative messages emanating from the candidates increase citizens' levels of knowledge. In contrast, negative messages originating from the press do not alter people's familiarity with the campaign. This may be the case because candidates' messages vary more dramatically in their tone than messages delivered by the press. For instance, it is not unusual, especially in competitive elections, for candidates to run exclusively negative advertisements. In races where polls show a horse race, particularly in the last few weeks of the campaign, candidates attack their opponents constantly in speeches, in press conferences, and certainly in their commercials. In contrast, in low-key races where incumbents lead by large margins, there are few if any negative messages present in the voters' environment, at least coming from incumbents.

Critical comments presented by the press do not typically vary as dramatically as those by candidates. The amount of negativity reported in the press, as captured by criticisms of the candidates, never exceeds 20 percent of total press coverage, even in the most intense races. It is possible, then, that the amount of negativity coming from the press is obscured by a wealth of additional information found in news stories.[39]

In the end, then, the findings from this chapter bring to light a conundrum of sorts. Citizens' familiarity with candidates and campaigns increases as campaigns become more unpleasant and malicious, compared to campaigns with no hint of mudslinging. Yet there is little sympathy and very little support among voters for mudslinging during campaigns. There is nearly universal disdain among citizens for nasty campaigns. It is hard to imagine calls by the public for harsher campaigns.

So, where does that leave us? Proponents of democratic elections discuss the importance of increasing citizens' understanding of political matters. But it appears that citizens' political sensibilities have to be accosted in order to increase their knowledge about campaigns. While harsh campaigns clearly enhance learning, we have yet to examine how voters use negative information when forming impressions of the candidates. Do citizens evaluate candidates differently based on the type of negative information they receive during campaigns? Does mudslinging lead to more critical evaluations of the competing candidates, compared to alternative forms of negative information? Are citizens more likely to stay home or are they more likely to go to the polls when campaign information is primarily negative? We turn to these questions in the next chapter.

NOTES

1. The survey data used in this chapter comes from the National Election Study Senate Election Study (1988–1992). Warren E. Miller, Donald R. Kinder, Steven J. Rosen Stone, and the National Election Studies, *National Election Studies*, 1988, 1990, 1992. Poolod Senate Election Study (Ann Arbor, MI: University of Michigan, Center for Political Studies, 1999). See Chapter 1 for more information about this dataset.
2. See, for example, the following studies: Kim F. Kahn and Patrick J. Kenney, *The Spectacle of U.S. Senate Campaigns* (Princeton, NJ: University of Princeton Press, 1999); Tracy Sulkin, "Campaign Intensity," *American Politics Research* 29 (1999): 608–624; Mark C. Westlye, *Senate Elections and Campaign Intensity* (Baltimore, MD: Johns Hopkins University Press, 1991).
3. See the following studies for more information about the greater salience of negative information: D. L. Hamilton and M. P. Zanna, "Context Effects in Impression Formation: Changes in Connotative Meaning," *Journal of Personality and Social Psychology* 29 (1974): 649–654; Karen S. Johnson-Cartee and Gary Copeland, "Southern Voters' Reaction to Negative Political Ads in 1986 Election," *Journalism Quarterly* 66 (1989): 188–193, 196; Richard Lau, "Two Explanations for Negativity Effects in Political Behavior," *American Journal of Political Science* 29 (1985): 119–138.
4. Susan T. Fiske, "Attention and Weight in Person Perception: The Impact of Negative and Extreme Behavior," *Journal of Personality and Social Psychology* 38 (1980): 889–906.
5. Felicia Pratto and Oliver P. John, "Automatic Vigilance: The Attention-Grabbing Power of Negative Social Information," *Journal of Personality and Social Psychology* 61 (1991): 380–391.
6. The following are a sample of studies finding greater differences in recall for negative advertisements, compared to positive advertisements: Craig L. Brians and Martin Wattenberg, "Campaign Issue Knowledge and Salience: Comparing Reception from TV Commercials, TV News, and Newspapers," *American Journal of Political Science* 40 (1996): 172–193; James B. Lemert, William R. Elliot, James M. Bernstein, William L. Rosenberg, and Karl J. Nestvold, *News Verdicts, the Debates, and Presidential Campaigns* (New York: Praeger (1991); John E. Newhagen and Byron Reeves, "Emotion and Memory Responses

for Negative Political Advertising: A Study of Television Commercials Used in the 1988 Presidential Election," in *Television and Political Advertising Volume 1: Psychological Processes*, ed. Frank Biocca (Hillsdale, NJ: Lawrence Erlbaum Associates, 1991); Marilyn Roberts, "Political Advertising: Strategies for Influence," in *Presidential Campaign Discourse: Strategic Communication Problems*, ed. Kathleen L. Kandall (Albany, NY: SUNY Press, 1995).

7. Daniel Kahneman and A. Tversky, "Choices, Values, and Frames," *American Psychologist* 39 (1984): 341–350; Richard Lau, "Negativity in Person Perception," *Political Behavior* 4 (1982): 353–377; Richard Lau, "Two Explanations for Negativity Effects in Political Behavior"; Kathleen M. McGraw and Marco Steenbergen, "Pictures in the Head: Memory Representation of Political Candidates," in *Political Judgment: Structure and Process*, ed. Milton Lodge and Kathleen M. McGraw (Ann Arbor, MI: The University of Michigan Press, 1997).

8. Tiffany A. Ito, Jeff T. Larsen, N. Kyle Smith, and John T. Cacioppo, "Negative Information Weighs More Heavily on the Brain: The Negativity Bias in Evaluative Categorizations," *Journal of Personality and Social Psychology* 75 (1998): 887–900.

9. See, for example, Michael Basil, Caroline Schooler, Byron Reeves, "Positive and Negative Political Advertising: Effectiveness of Ads and Perceptions of Candidates," in *Television and Political Advertising, Volume 1: Psychological Processes*, ed. Frank Biocca (Hillsdale, NJ: Lawrence Erlbaum Associates, 1991); Craig L. Brians and Martin Wattenberg, "Campaign Issue Knowledge and Salience: Comparing Reception from TV News, TV Commercials, and Newspapers," *American Journal of Political Science* 40 (1996): 172–193; Kim Fridkin Kahn and John G. Geer, "Creating Impressions: An Experimental Investigation of the Effectiveness of Television Advertising," *Political Behavior* 16 (1994): 93–115; Martin Wattenberg and Craig Brians, "Negative Campaign Advertising: Demobilizer or Mobilizer," *American Political Science Review* 93 (1999): 877–890.

10. See Amy Guttmann, "The Disharmony of Democracy," in *Democratic Community*, ed. John W. Chapman and Ian Shapiro (New York: New York University Press, 1993); and Kim Fridkin Kahn and Patrick J. Kenney, "Do Negative Campaigns Mobilize or Suppress Turnout? Clarifying the Relationship between Negativity and Participation," *American Political Science Review* 93 (1999): 877–890.

11. Kim F. Kahn and Patrick J. Kenney, "Do Negative Campaigns Mobilize or Suppress Turnout?" See also Kathleen Hall Jamieson, *Everything You Think You Know About Politics— and Why You're Wrong* (New York: Basic Books, 2000).

12. Kahn and Kenney find that 10 percent of races exhibit extreme mudslinging, while another 20 percent experience moderate mudslinging. Kim Fridkin Kahn and Patrick J. Kenney, "Do Negative Campaigns Mobilize or Suppress Turnout?"

13. Doris Kearns Goodwin, *The Fitzgeralds and the Kennedys* (New York: St. Martins Press, 1987).

14. We have discussed only a few of the various allegations and potential scandals in the campaign. There were charges of "dirty trick" emails. Grams was hounded by the possibility of an illicit affair. Grams's son's arrests were discussed extensively during the campaign. And "ad watches" by Minneapolis and St. Paul newspapers found little accuracy in many of the candidates' ads, with special attention directed at Dayton's accusations of Grams. In other words, the mudslinging was a constant feature of this campaign.

15. The first systematic studies of campaign effects were published almost sixty years ago: Paul Lazarsfeld, Bernard Berelson, and Hazel Gaude, *The People's Choice* (New York: Columbia University Press, 1944); Bernard Berelson, Paul Lazarsfeld, and William McPhee, *Voting: A Study of Opinion Formation in a Presidential Campaign* (Chicago, IL: University of Chicago Press, 1954).

16. Richard R. Lau, Lee Sigelman, Caroline Heldman, and Paul Babbitt, "The Effects of Negative Political Advertisements: A Meta-Analytic Assessment," *American Political Science Review* 93 (1999): 851–876.

17. For a detailed review of this literature see Richard R. Lau and Lee Sigelman, "Effectiveness of Negative Political Advertising," in *Crowded Airwaves: Campaign Advertising in Elections*, ed. James A. Thurber, Candice J. Nelson, and David A. Dulio (Washington, D.C.: Brookings Institution Press, 2000).

18. For one exception, see Kim F. Kahn and Patrick J. Kenney, "How Negative Campaigning Enhances Knowledge of Senate Elections," in *Crowded Airwaves: Campaign Advertising in Elections*, ed. James A. Thurber, Candice J. Nelson, and David A. Dulio (Washington, D.C.: Brookings Institution Press, 2000).

19. See Kim F. Kahn and Patrick J. Kenney, *The Spectacle of U.S. Senate Campaigns*.
20. See Appendix A for details about the measurement of these variables.
21. For evidence supporting the discrepancy hypothesis, see Richard Lau, "Two Explanations for Negativity Effects in Political Behavior," *American Journal of Political Science* 29 (1985): 119–138; Robert M. Reyes, William C. Thompson, and Gordon H. Bower, "Judgmental Biases Resulting from Differing Availability of Arguments," *Journal of Personality and Social Psychology* 39 (1980): 2–12; Eliot R. Smith and Frederick D. Miller, "Salience and the Cognitive Mediation of Attribution," *Journal of Personality and Social Psychology* 37 (1979): 2240–2252.
22. Phillip E. Converse, "Nature of Belief Systems in Mass Publics," in *Ideology and Discontent*, ed. David Apter (New York: Free Press, 1964); Michael X. Deli Carpini and Scott Keeter, *What Americans Know about Politics and Why It Matters* (New Haven, CT: Yale University Press, 1996).
23. See Craig Leonard Brians and Martin P. Wattenberg, "Campaign Issue Knowledge and Salience: Comparing Reception from TV Commercials, TV News, and Newspapers," *American Journal of Political Science* 40 (1996): 172–193.
24. See Jon K. Dalager, "Voters, Issues, and Elections: Are the Candidates' Messages Getting Through?" *The Journal of Politics* 58 (1996): 486–515; Jack M. McLeod and Daniel McDonald, "Beyond Simple Exposure: Media Orientations and Their Impact on Political Processes," *Communication Research* 12 (1985): 3–34; Michael J. Robinson and Dennis K. Davis, "Television News and the Informed Public," *Journal of Communication* 40 (1990): 106–119.
25. See Steven J. Rosenstone and John Mark Hansen, *Mobilization, Participation, and Democracy in America* (New York: Macmillan Publishing Company, 1993).
26. For information about the importance of strength of partisanship, see Warren E. Miller and J. Merrill Shanks, *The New American Voter* (Cambridge, MA: Harvard University Press, 1996).
27. The measure is the number of negative advertisements aired by each candidate divided by the total number of advertisements aired by the candidate. The incumbent (and winners in open races) measure of negative advertisements has a mean of .22 and a standard deviation of .26. The challenger (and losers in open races) has a mean of .40 and a standard deviation of .34.
28. The measure of press negativity for incumbents (and winners in open races) has a mean of .11 and a standard deviation of .06. The measure of press negativity for challengers (and losers in open races) has a mean of .09 and a standard deviation of .07
29. Kathleen Hall Jamieson also makes this distinction in her book, *Everything You Think You Know About Politics—and Why You're Wrong*.
30. The question posed to managers was: What are the main themes of your opponent's campaign? If neither manager described the opponent as engaging in "mudslinging," the race received a score of 0; if one manager described the opponent as engaging in "mudslinging," the race received a score of 1; if both candidates viewed their opponent as having run a "mudslinging" campaign, the race received a score of 2.
31. The measure ranges from 0 (indicating the respondent was never exposed to the candidate across the three media) to 3 (indicating the respondent recalls seeing the candidate on television, hearing about the candidate on the radio, and reading about the candidate in the newspaper).
32. There is a wealth of research demonstrating that any type of spending enhances the campaign prospects of challengers. See, for example, Gary C. Jacobson, *The Politics of Congressional Elections*, 5th ed. (New York: Longman Press, 2000).
33. Larry M. Bartels, *Presidential Primaries and the Dynamics of Public Choice* (Princeton, NJ: Princeton University Press, 1988); Gary C. Jacobson, *The Politics of Congressional Elections* (New York: Longman, 1997).
34. The exact wording of the question is, "I'll read the name of a person and I'd like you to rate that person using something called the feeling thermometer. You can choose any number from 0 to 100. The higher the number, the warmer or more favorable you feel toward that person; the lower the number, the colder or less favorable. You would rate the person at the 50 degree mark if you feel neither warm nor cold toward them."
35. Richard F. Fenno, *Senators on the Campaign Trail* (Norman, OK: University of Oklahoma Press, 1996).
36. Respondents who identify a negative theme of the campaign are coded 1, while the rest of the sample are coded 0.

37. We use the campaign manager surveys to identify the candidates' main themes. Respondents that correctly identified the candidates' main campaign themes were coded 1, while all remaining respondents were coded 0.
38. In this analysis, we hold all remaining variables in the models in Table 4.3 at their means while varying the amount of negative information.
39. While the tone of press coverage does not matter, the overall amount of press coverage does influence voters' awareness of the campaign. We replicated the analyses in Tables 4.1–4.3 including a variable measuring the total amount of press coverage. The measure of amount of press coverage is statistically significant in each of the equations.

5

DOES NEGATIVITY SHAPE
CITIZENS' BELIEFS AND BEHAVIOR?

For the last third of the twentieth century, the heart-rending issue of abortion has vexed the American people and their representatives. Finding a solution for unwanted pregnancies that all citizens find acceptable has proven illusive. Highly organized and well-financed political groups have staked ground on opposite sides of the abortion issue. Legislatures, executives, and courts throughout the federal system have legislated, directed, and ruled on various aspects of the abortion issue in an attempt to create a coherent policy. Yet every governmental decision is applauded by some citizens and criticized by others. Riveted at the center of the dilemma are the intertwined and often competing concepts of "life, liberty and the pursuit of happiness." At least for the foreseeable future, the problem appears intractable and a compromise solution seems a distant and remote possibility.

The U.S. Senate, for better or worse, entered this fray in the spring of 1997. In May of 1997, Senator Rick Santorum, a Republican from Pennsylvania, sponsored a measure that banned the controversial procedure known by the public as "partial-birth abortion." Similar legislation had passed the House in March of 1997 by a vote of 295–136. The proposed law would prohibit this gut-wrenching procedure. Proponents of the bill argued the procedure was "infanticide." Opponents of the ban argued that the procedure should be available to women when their lives are in grave danger. Debate on the floor of the U.S. Senate was strident, at times inflammatory, but always emotional. On May 20, the Senate approved the ban by a vote of 64–36.

These types of votes, beyond distressing the hearts and souls of legislators, can directly influence their political futures. One-third of the senators voting on the bill faced election in eighteen months. Two Democrats, Senator Russell Feingold of Wisconsin and Senator Bob Graham of Florida, voted against the ban. Both were seeking reelection in the fall of 1998. Both would win. But Feingold's vote would become a campaign issue, the focus of numerous negative attacks by his challenger. Graham's vote, on the other hand, would go largely unchallenged by his opponent. These two races illustrate how differences in campaigns, specifically differences in negative campaigns, can alter the dynamics of elections in terms of citizens' participation in the election as well as their evaluations of the competing candidates.

Feingold ran into stiff competition in the election of 1998.[1] Congressman Mark Neumann, first elected in 1994 when the Republicans captured the House of Representatives, was eager to become a U.S. senator. Neumann had resources and he targeted Feingold as early as 1997. Both candidates spent approximately 4 million to win the race; Feingold spent a little under 4 million and Neumann spent a little over. The campaign included discussions on a range of issues, such as social security, education, taxes, defense, and the environment. And the campaign featured rhetoric about "partial birth abortion." Neumann supported the ban in the House of Representatives and criticized Feingold's vote in May of 1997. By the fall campaign of 1998, he attacked Feingold on his vote and challenged him to explain his position. He brought attention to the issue through his advertising campaign. At every turn, Neumann explained in some detail the nature of the partial-birth procedure and described Feingold as an "extremist on the abortion issue generally." In addition, the National Pro-Life Association targeted Feingold and ran commercials discussing his vote "in favor" of the partial-birth procedure.

Feingold did not flinch from his position; he restated that he could not support a ban unless the life of the mother was specifically protected. Feingold and his supporters delivered several attacks against Neumann. During a head-to-head debate in late October, Feingold criticized Neumann for raising the issue so frequently. Feingold accused Neumann of describing the partial-birth procedure "for the shock value—over and over again, so he can get as many votes as he can off it." The Democratic Party ran 211 ads against Neumann, all negative in tone. Several other political groups ran a total of 71 ads against Neumann, again all negative.

Polls in late October indicated the race was extremely close. On election day, Feingold captured 51 percent of the vote to Neumann's 48 percent. Forty-four percent of the voting age population came to the polls in Wisconsin in 1998, compared to the national average of 38 percent for this off-year election. And, turnout in the Feingold-Neumann election was higher than in Wisconsin's previous senatorial race in 1994, where 41 percent of the voting-age-population came out to the polls. Did more people vote because of the emotional discussions on the partial-birth issue? Several newspaper articles in late October of 1998, published in different papers across Wisconsin, speculated about the possibility that turnout may be heightened in the 1998 race because "pro-life" groups would mobilize their followers to vote against Feingold.[2]

Exit polls suggested that Neumann's negative critiques about Feingold's vote on the partial-birth abortion issue made a difference to some voters. In fact, according to data collected by the Voter News Service, 20 percent of voters said that abortion was the "top issue in their Senate vote." Only Social

Security was considered the top issue by more voters, and then by only six percent. Of those 20 percent that focused on abortion, 82 percent voted for Neumann.

While voters turned out in large numbers in Wisconsin in 1998, turnout in Florida was significantly lower, with only 33 percent of the voting age population going to the polls. In Florida, Senator Bob Graham was coasting to victory over state legislator Charlie Crist. Graham outspent Crist nearly five to one, Graham ran three times more ads than Crist, and Graham, not Crist, aired negative ads, but only a few. In addition, neither party nor interest groups ran commercials, either positive or negative. Graham's 1997 vote on the partial birth abortion was not a topic of the campaign and was not discussed in any significant way. Graham captured 63 percent of the vote and Crist managed 38 percent.

Exit polls did not detect any issues that were on the minds of Florida voters in 1998, with the possible exception of school vouchers. The citizens of Florida were concerned most about the personal qualities of the candidates, such as honesty, effectiveness, ability to bring change, and experience. On each of these qualities, Graham was looked on more favorably than Crist, by wide margins. This was not a campaign with meaningful discussion of policy proposals, and voters' reactions to the candidates reflected this lack of substance.

It appears that the vote on abortion nearly cost Feingold his job; yet the same vote posed absolutely no problem for Graham. Why? One possible explanation is that citizens' views on abortion were starkly different in Florida and Wisconsin. However, this does not seem to be the case. First, in the spring of 1997, the state legislatures in Florida and Wisconsin were passing legislation banning partial-birth abortions. Both houses in the Florida legislature passed the ban that spring, and the Assembly in Wisconsin passed the ban in May. The votes in both states were by large margins. So state legislatures in both states, representing thousands and thousands of constituents, were passing nearly identical pieces of legislation.

Second, newspapers in both states ran a substantial number of articles discussing the Senate's actions and their senators' votes. Third, both prospective challengers, Neumann and Crist, criticized the senators in May of 1997. Neumann, quoted in an article in the *Milwaukee Journal Sentinel* on May 22, 1997, claimed, "[Feingold] turned a blind eye to the most vulnerable and innocent among us." Crist, quoted in an article in the *Sarasota Herald-Tribune* on May 25, 1997, stated, "I think it [Graham's vote] just illustrates a blind, unthinking devotion to the political correctness of the fringe elements of his party."

Fourth, NES/SES survey data indicates citizens in these states held similar views about abortion. Approximately one-quarter of the people of Wisconsin and Florida believe abortion should be legal under "any circumstances," about one-half believe abortion should be legal under "certain circumstances," and less than 15 percent believe abortion should "never be legal." Citizens' responses to the NES/SES question on abortion were nearly identical. In the end, then, differences in the role of abortion in these campaigns cannot be explained by the differences in public opinion or the political climate.

Instead, the role of abortion in these two campaigns may reflect differences in the use of negative messages by the candidates. Neumann, with resources, tenacity, and skill kept Feingold the target of criticism throughout the campaign. Crist, without resources, and with limited campaign skills and low name recognition, could not keep any viable issue on the campaign agenda, let alone Graham's vote on the partial-birth abortion. Relying on the Wisconsin and Florida campaigns in 1998 as points of departure, we move to a systematic examination of how negative messages influence voters' likelihood of voting and affect their evaluations of competing candidates.

INTEREST IN CAMPAIGNS

Political scientists have gathered approximately a half-century of data on people's interest in politics generally and people's interest in campaigns specifically. Approximately one-third of the electorate responds that they are "very interested" in campaigns during presidential campaigns, and approximately one-quarter of the population claims to be "very interested" in campaigns during mid-term elections.[3]

Citizens' levels of interest should be related to the content and tone of campaign information. At the very least, critical information focusing on important and emotional issues, such as abortion, should heighten citizens' interest in the outcome of elections. If candidates are staking ground and criticizing their opponents on hotly debated issues and if the news media cover these exchanges, then voters are likely to become more interested in the campaign. As we discussed in Chapter 4, negative information tends to be more readily remembered by individuals. And criticisms, such as in an advertisement, or during a debate, or in a news article may provide useful information to voters.

However, when the negative messages in the campaign turn nasty, that is, criticisms focus on irrelevant topics and are presented in an discourteous fashion, interest in the campaign may decline. In other words, when campaign discourse degenerates into mudslinging, voters are likely to lose interest in the election.

Beyond campaign information, however, researchers have noted that citizens' interest in campaigns varies according to at least three forces: the personal characteristics of voters, such as strength of attachment to a political party; the importance of the political office, such as presidential campaigns versus congressional campaigns; the characteristics of campaigns, such as the amount of media coverage or the salience of issues.[4] Even after these forces are taken into account, interest among voters should increase when negative information is presented about relevant topics in an appropriate manner. And, not surprisingly, interest in campaigns should decline when criticisms degenerate into mudslinging.

To measure interest in the campaign, we relied on the NES/SES question: "Some people don't pay much attention to political campaigns. How about you? Would you say that you were very much interested, somewhat interested, or not much interested?" This measure of interest does not ask respondents specifically about interest in senatorial campaigns. Instead, the question inquires about interest in "political campaigns" generally. Thus, to isolate interest in senatorial races, we examine only the 1990 campaigns. Senatorial campaigns held in the off-year do not compete with presidential campaigns for voters' interest and attention. If we use respondents' answers in 1988 and 1992, we cannot sort out whether a response of "very much interested" in the campaign refers to the presidential or senatorial campaign. We remove the confounding influence of the presidential campaigns by examining only 1990.

We employ the same three measures of negativity that were used in Chapter 4: the proportion of negative advertisements aired by the candidates, the proportion of critical paragraphs printed about each candidate in newspapers, and the presence of mudslinging in the race. To assess properly the relationship between negative information and interest, we consider the traditional explanations known to affect interest in campaigns: the characteristics of the race (i.e., spending by the candidates, competition, open versus incumbent races), the characteristics of the candidates (i.e., seniority, challenger quality, gender), the characteristics of the citizens (i.e., party attachment, education, attention to the news, sophistication).[5]

While looking at off-year elections eliminates the potential "contamination" of the presidential campaign, it does not eliminate the potential "contamination" of gubernatorial races contested during the off-year. After all, many gubernatorial races are the headline-making campaigns in the state. Therefore, when looking at interest in campaigns in 1990, we need to assess the characteristics of the gubernatorial races contested during the campaign season. First, we note if there is a gubernatorial race in the state concurrent with a U.S. Senate campaign. Second, we measure the closeness of the gubernatorial races.[6] Third, we assess the negativity of the gubernatorial campaign by measuring the tone of front page news coverage of these races.

Sure enough, negative information has two significant and distinct effects on levels of interest in campaigns. Mudslinging decreases citizens' interest in political campaigns (see Table 5.1). When campaigns degenerate into mudslinging, potential voters lose interest in the political spectacle. But, in contrast, criticisms in the press increase interest in campaigns (see Table 5.1). Useful negative information generated by the news media (i.e., criticisms of the candidates) heightens interest among voters. The critical coverage in the press has an impressive impact on political interest. In fact, as the proportion

TABLE 5.1   THE IMPACT OF NEGATIVE INFORMATION
ON VOTER INTEREST IN SENATE CAMPAIGNS

	UNSTANDARDIZED LOGIT COEFFICIENT (STANDARD ERROR)	BETA
Negative Campaign Information		
Candidates' Ads	−.03 (.26)	−.01
Press Criticisms of Candidates	2.77 (1.17)**	.07
Mudslinging	−.09 (.05)*	−.04
Characteristics of the Race		
Campaign Spending	−.01 (.03)	−.01
Competition	−.001 (.003)	−.02
Open	−.15 (.18)	−.03
Characteristics of the Candidates		
Seniority	.01 (.004)***	.07
Challenger Quality	.005 (.005)	.02
Gender	−.11 (.07)	−.03
Other Campaigns		
Presence of Gubernatorial Campaign	.02 (.23)	.01
Closeness of Gubernatorial Campaign	.005 (.04)	.01
Tone of Gubernatorial Campaign	.05 (.06)	.04
Characteristics of Citizens		
Strength of Partisanship	.14 (.03)***	.10
Education	.03 (.01)***	.06
Attention to News	.09 (.007)***	.25
Sophistication	.25 (.02)***	.28
Intercept	−5.27 (.28)***	

N = 2304
R^2 = .23
***$p < .01$
**$p < .05$
*$p < .10$
The p-values are based on two-tailed tests.

of negative press coverage increases from virtually zero to over one-third of all coverage, voters' interest in campaigns can vary as much as one full category on the three-point interest scale (e.g., moving from "somewhat interested" to "very much interested"). Indeed, the criticisms in the press have a stronger influence on interest than respondents' levels education, the amount of money spent in the race, or the closeness of the senate contest.[7]

The remaining measure of negativity—proportion of negative ads aired by the candidates—fails to have a significant impact on political interest. Also, the characteristics of the race (e.g., competition, amount of spending, type of race) do not influence political interest. Similarly the quality of the challenger and the gender of the candidate fail to affect people's level of political interest. However, people express greater interest in campaigns when the sitting senator is more senior.

Citizens' characteristics (e.g., how often they pay attention to the media, their attachment to the parties) strongly influence their interest in campaigns. The most important factor predicting individuals' interest in politics is their general levels of sophistication about politics.

Our results suggest that the tone of campaigns, although not the only important factor explaining citizens' interest, has a strong influence on why some people are very interested in campaigns while others do not care much at all. Campaigns with large amounts of mudslinging produce an electorate less interested in politics. On the other hand, campaigns with a plethora of legitimate criticisms presented by the press can enhance voters' interest in campaigns.

VOTER TURNOUT IN NEGATIVE CAMPAIGNS

Beyond influencing interest in elections, the tone of campaigns may mobilize citizens to vote or dissuade citizens from participating in elections. Some scholars have argued that when candidates engage in "mudslinging," citizens become alienated from the electoral process and stay home on election day.[8] Negative campaign information may demobilize the electorate because it increases voter disgust and alienation toward the competing candidates and the political process. Thus, over time, negative campaigns may pose a threat to a healthy democracy because citizens fail to participate in the process of determining who holds power and for how long.

Other scholars, however, present reasons why negative campaigns may enhance turnout, especially compared to positively oriented campaigns.[9] For instance, negative advertising may heighten turnout because negative messages provide people with reasons why they should support one candidate over another. This line of reasoning fits nicely with the discussion in Chapter 4 where we noted that citizens automatically notice and process negative information that relates to their well-being.

We, too, are interested in the impact of negativity on participation. In an earlier investigation, we pointed out that not all negative messages are the same.[10] Consequently, scholars should not expect different types of negative messages to have the same impact on citizens' propensity to vote. Negative messages, especially compared to positive appeals, generate more involvement in campaigns when they emphasize legitimate issues or relevant personality characteristics and are presented in a civil manner. Campaigns with these types of critical messages will experience higher turnout on election day.

However, when negative messages center on questionable topics and are presented in an illegitimate fashion, citizens become alienated. As we discussed in Chapter 4, certain campaign topics are simply inappropriate; they do not resonate well with voters. Likewise, if candidates criticize their opponents in an improper fashion (e.g., using an overly strident tone), citizens may become uncomfortable with the campaign and the candidates. In these situations, we expect voters to disengage and to stay home.

To marshal evidence for this claim, we examined the relationship between different types of negativity and turnout in the 1990 senate elections. As with interest, we examined 1990 in order to stay away from the confounding influence of the presidential campaigns in 1988 and 1992.[11] We included the same three measures of negativity introduced earlier in this chapter: the proportion of negative ads, the proportion of criticisms in the press, and the amount of mudslinging.

We found that the negativity of the ads, the negativity of news coverage, and the presence of "mudslinging" each influence turnout, but in different ways (see Appendix B). In particular, people are more likely to vote as negative information increases in the candidates' advertisements and in the press, holding a host of rival forces constant.[12] Mudslinging, in contrast, and as expected, depresses turnout. Voters exposed to "mudslinging" campaigns are less likely to vote in senate elections (see Appendix B). These results suggest that people distinguish between legitimate and tempered criticisms, on the one hand, and acrimonious and unjust criticisms, on the other hand. Voters seem to find substantive and reasonable criticisms useful, actually providing them with reasons to go to the polls. In contrast, excessive "mudslinging" alienates voters, and citizens withdraw from the electoral process by staying home on election day.

The distinction between legitimate negative information and mudslinging moves us a long way toward understanding why some people vote during negative campaigns and others do not. Still, does negative information affect all people equally? In other words, are negative messages useful for some voters but of little value to others? Does mudslinging offend some citizens more sharply than others? We believe the answers to these questions lie with the characteristics of the citizens.

Some citizens are motivated to vote because of long-standing personal characteristics.[13] These habitual voters are likely to participate in elections regardless of the tone of the campaign rhetoric. Similarly, citizens vary widely in their interest and knowledge about politics.[14] People with more information about politics and more interest in political matters are less likely to be influenced by the tone of political campaigns. Finally, some individuals have the time and resources to actively take part in politics and they are not likely to be deterred as a result of the tone of campaign messages.[15]

In contrast to people with the skills, sophistication, and resources to vote, the bulk of the electorate are only marginally involved in the political world.[16] They have little interest in elections, they are not linked psychologically to one of the parties, they are unlikely to know very much about politics, they live on the margins of society, and they tend not to believe they have a stake in the political process.[17] Most of these citizens have a predisposition *not* to vote. So, campaigns that provide serious and contentious dialogue in a thoughtful and civil manner may actually grab the attention of uninformed and uninterested voters. These campaigns may generate reasons for these people to participate. However, the positive effects of negative discourse disappear in a hurry when campaigns degenerate into mudslinging. If candidates debase the political process with shrill and irrelevant commentary, then people already predisposed to stay home will skip elections altogether.

To determine if the relationship between negative information and turnout is affected by the individual characteristics of citizens, we divide people into groups based on their psychological attachment to a party, their interest in politics, their level of political sophistication, and their race or income. Indeed, once the electorate is subdivided into to these groups, we find strong support for the idea that negative information does not affect all people equally. The relationship between negative information and turnout is conditioned dramatically by people's personal characteristics.[18]

Specifically, partisans, politically interested citizens, political experts, and white citizens with moderate and comfortable incomes are largely unaffected by the negativity of campaign messages (see Table 5.2).[19] Legitimate critical information presented via newspapers and political advertisements does not significantly increase turnout among these citizens. Furthermore, mudslinging plays absolutely no role in changing the likelihood that these people will go to the polls. Strong partisans, people who are interested and knowledgeable about politics, and people with resources go to the polls. They are not motivated or deterred by negative rhetoric.

The results are strikingly different for independents, citizens with little interest in campaigns, persons lacking stored information about politics, and people living on the margins of society. These individuals are much more susceptible to the tone of campaigns. Useful critical information, particularly information presented by the press, significantly increases their probability of voting. Political novices, for example, are more likely to vote as the proportion of useful negative messages increases in candidates' ads and in the press. They find both streams of negative commentary helpful. Indeed, each group of voters responds positively to either ads or the press. As useful negative commentary increases from one of these two sources, typical nonvoters are more likely to cast ballots.

In addition, these citizens react strongly to "mudslinging." Their probability of voting consistently and significantly *decreases* when campaigns disintegrate into "mudslinging" contests. People on the margins of the political

TABLE 5.2 THE INFLUENCE OF NEGATIVE INFORMATION ON TURNOUT:
THE IMPORTANCE OF CITIZEN CHARACTERISTICS

	NEGATIVITY OF ADS	CRITICISMS IN THE PRESS	MUDSLINGING
Partisans (n = 1288)	.16 (.09)**	.84 (1.44)	−.06 (.05)
Very Interested (n = 732)	.18 (.14)	2.22 (2.35)	−.10 (.08)
Political Experts (n = 788)	−.04 (.13)	2.37 (2.35)	−.05 (.07)
Whites or Not Poor (n = 1519)	.01 (.08)	2.63 (1.35)**	−.05 (.04)
Independents (n = 968)	.11 (.09)	3.20 (1.62)***	−.11 (.06)**
Not Very Interested (n = 1524)	.11 (.07)	2.45 (1.19)***	−.08 (.04)***
Political Novices (n = 1468)	.19 (.07)***	2.19 (1.22)***	−.09 (.04)***
Minority or Poor (n = 737)	.28 (.10)***	1.98 (1.89)	−.11 (.06)**

In each cell, we present the unstandardized logit coefficient followed by the standard error in parentheses. In the logit equations predicting turnout, we control for the following variables: closeness of the campaign, presence of governor's race, negativity of governor's race, closeness of governor's race, proportion of competitive House races, difference in evaluation of the candidates, favorability toward the candidates, contact with incumbent/open winner, contact with challenger/open loser, exposure to incumbent/open winner, exposure to challenger/open loser, knowledge of incumbent/open winner, knowledge of challenger/open loser, mention of campaign theme, age of respondent, age^2, employment status, home ownership, length of residency, and residency in South.

Respondents were classified as *Independents* or *Partisans* based on their answer to the "root" party identification question. We relied on the political interest question to classify people as *Low in Political Interest* (respondents who said they were "somewhat interested" or "not much interested" in political campaigns) or *High in Political Interest* (respondents who said they were "very much interested" in political campaigns). We developed a measure of political sophistication to assess people's levels of political information. Based on answers to six questions available in the NES/SES, we divide respondents into two categories: *Political Novices* (respondents correctly answering zero to four of the knowledge questions) and *Political Experts* (respondents correctly answering five to six of the knowledge questions). Finally, *Minority/Poor* are African-Americans, Hispanics, or people whose families made less than $20,000 a year, while *Whites/Not Poor* are whites or people whose families made $20,000 a year or more.

All p-values are two-tailed.

***p < .01

**p < .05

*p < .10

world have little tolerance for campaigns devoid of useful content. When bombarded with shrill and irrelevant messages by the candidates, independents, uninterested citizens, uniformed Americans, minorities, and the poor stay home on election day.

To demonstrate the importance of mudslinging for decreasing turnout among these subpopulations, we vary the presence of mudslinging and estimate the probability that these citizens will go to the polls on election day (see Figure 5.1 on page 98). For each group, the probability of voting decreases in the presence of mudslinging. For some groups, the changes in the likelihood of voting are dramatic. For instance, among minority or poor citizens, the chances of voting on election day drops by ten points in races filled with mudslinging, all things being equal. Similarly, political novices

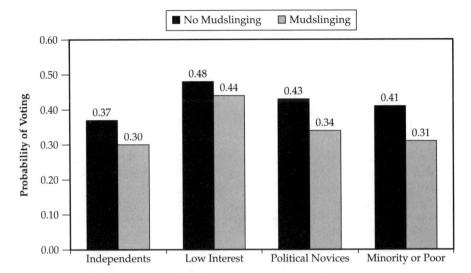

FIGURE 5.1   THE IMPACT OF MUDSLINGING ON TURNOUT

Note: Probabilities are derived from the logit estimates presented in Appendix B.
Source: Kahn and Kenney's data and NES/SES data.

are particularly sensitive to mudslinging. When mudslinging is absent, novices have a .43 chance of turning out to vote in senate elections. However, when candidates engage in mudslinging, the probability that novices will vote drops to .34.

These results demonstrate clearly that certain types of citizens are sensitive to negative campaigning, while other citizens are far less responsive. Given these results, we decided to investigate whether the content of campaign information influences the voting behavior of the nations' largest subpopulation—women. Women and men may react differently to negative information because they are socialized differently.[20] From an early age, girls are taught that passivity is a desired trait and aggressive behavior should be avoided. Boys, on the other hand, are encouraged to be aggressive and passivity is seen as a weakness. If these lessons of childhood persist into adulthood, women may be less receptive than men to antagonistic and belligerent campaign techniques, such as negative campaigning.[21]

Indeed, the impact of critical campaign information differs for men and women (see Table 5.3). Negative information presented by the press and the candidates mobilize male respondents. As the proportion of critical news and negative advertisements escalates, men are more likely to go to the polls on election day. To illustrate the importance of negative information for men, we vary the amount of negativity in the news and in the candidates' advertisements, and estimate turnout rates for male respondents. When the negative

**Table 5.3   The Influence of Negative Information
on Turnout: The Importance of Gender**

Proportion of Negative Information	Men	Women
Candidates' Ads	.27 (.10)***	.05 (.08)
Press Criticisms of Candidates	1.55 (.79)***	.05 (.72)
Mudslinging	−.09 (.05)**	−.10 (.05)***

In each cell, we present the unstandardized logit coefficient followed by the standard error in parentheses. In the logit equations predicting turnout, we control for the following variables: closeness of the campaign, presence of governor's race, negativity of governor's race, closeness of governor's race, proportion of competitive House races, difference in evaluation of the candidates, favorability toward the candidates, contact with incumbent/open winner, contact with challenger/open loser, exposure to incumbent/open winner, exposure to challenger/open loser, knowledge of incumbent/open winner, knowledge of challenger/open loser, mention of campaign theme, education level of respondent, age of respondent, age^2, income, employment status, home ownership, length of residency, residency in South, partisan attachment, interest in campaigns.

All p-values are two-tailed.

***p < .01
**p < .05
*p < .10

content in the news and in the ads is minimal, men have a .56 probability of turning out to vote. However, when the amount of critical information reaches its peak, the probability of voting among male respondents jumps to .73. These results suggest that male respondents find this type of negative information useful, providing them with additional incentives that push them to the polls.

In stark contrast, negative information presented by the news and via the candidates' advertisements does not motivate women to get out and vote. Critical content in the news and in advertisements fail to encourage women to go to the polls. Women, unlike men, are less likely to see the utility of such negative information. Finally, both male and female respondents are "turned off" when campaigns are mudslinging affairs. As mudslinging increases, men and women are significantly less likely to vote.

The findings in this chapter influence our understanding of the nature of the U.S. electorate. Resourceful, interested, and informed partisans find their way to the polls, irrespective of the content of the candidates' messages. Their counterparts, however, are affected far more dramatically by the content and tone of negative information. Uninterested, uninformed, poor, and minority citizens are motivated to vote if they witness useful negative commentary, but stay home in mudslinging contests. Negative information also cuts across gender. Men are more likely than women to go to the polls when candidates provide meaningful criticisms. However, both men and women are more likely to skip voting if the candidates are involved in mean-spirited shenanigans. In the end, though, are the evaluations of potential voters influenced by negative information? We turn to this question next.

CITIZENS' EVALUATIONS OF CANDIDATES

Thus far we have seen that negative campaign messages alter the attitudes (i.e., interest in campaigns) and behaviors of citizens (i.e., likelihood of voting). However, one crucial question remains: Do negative messages alter people's evaluations of the candidates? Candidates launching negative messages have two goals in mind. At the very least, they intend to lower citizens' evaluations of opponents. In addition, candidates hope to increase voters' evaluations of their own candidacies.

To determine if these goals are realized, we need measures of citizens' evaluations of incumbents and challengers. We rely on the feeling thermometer introduced in Chapter 4 to determine if negative campaign messages affect how citizens evaluate candidates. When evaluating voters' evaluations of senate candidates, we are able to use the entire NES/SES sample from 1988–1992. In the survey, citizens were asked to evaluate the senatorial candidates by name. Thus, contamination from the presidential campaign is much less a problem than it was in the analyses of interest and turnout. In addition, as we discuss later, we are able to control for possible confounding effects of the presidential campaign much more effectively in this analysis.

To properly assess the relationship between negative messages and evaluations, we account for four forces known to affect respondents' evaluations of candidates: the quality of the candidates (e.g., seniority of senators), the characteristics of the campaign (e.g., campaign spending of the candidates), the political predispositions of the voters (e.g., party identification of the respondent), and the prevailing national political forces (e.g., the health of the economy). If negative campaign information influences citizens' evaluations of candidates when we include these competing forces, we can be reasonably confident that negative campaigns do "matter." Thus, the tone of information disseminated by the press and the candidates shapes how voters feel about competing candidates.

To measure the quality of the candidates, we include three indicators to capture the candidates' experience and talents. Among incumbents seeking reelection, senior senators are more successful in generating favorable ratings compared to their junior counterparts.[22] For challengers, we expect candidates with previous political "experience" and candidates who are "skillful campaigners" to receive higher scores than neophytes with minimal campaign abilities.[23] Finally, we take into account the gender of the candidate.

To capture the characteristics of the campaign, we incorporated measures of the amount of money spent by the candidates and the level of competition in the race. Candidates that spend more money traditionally receive higher scores on the feeling thermometers.[24] The competitiveness of the campaign may also influence voters' evaluations of candidates.[25]

We measure three political attitudes known to shape voters' evaluations: party identification, ideological characteristics, and assessments of issues. Voters routinely score candidates that share their party affiliation higher on the feeling thermometers.[26] In addition, voters nearly always evaluate candidates higher on the thermometers when they agree on ideological and issue matters.[27]

Finally, we know voters consider the prevailing national conditions when casting ballots. People who view the national economy as getting worse may blame candidates of the president's party. On the other hand, citizens who see the nation's economy as healthy may credit candidates who share the president's party.[28] Also, there is the possibility that attitudes about the president influence evaluations of senate candidates. The "coattail effect" suggests that voters simply use their vote for the president as a guide in their choice of senate candidates.[29] In addition, there is a possibility of "referendum voting." This idea suggests that voters may support the senate candidate of the president's party if they approve of the president's job performance. We control for this possibility by examining whether approval of the president is related to overall evaluations of the senate candidates.[30]

With various rival explanations in place, we examine directly the relationship between negative campaign messages and voters' evaluations of candidates. Consistent with prior analyses, we employ measures of negativity that capture mudslinging, the content of candidates' ads, and the proportion of criticisms in the press. We expect mudslinging to decrease evaluations of both incumbents and challengers. As we discussed at some length, we expect citizens to find little value in harsh messages. We expect that citizens will resent the candidates who engage in mudslinging. Likewise, criticisms in the press should decrease evaluations of incumbents and challengers. A steady stream of critical comments by reporters and editors may lead citizens to develop less favorable views of the candidates criticized in the press.

The effects of candidates' ads, on the other hand, are less clear-cut. Tempered and relevant attacks by candidates should decrease the opponents' evaluations. If candidates are persuasive in presenting reasons why voters should avoid their opponents in their advertisements, then citizens' evaluations of candidates' opponents should decrease. However, there are at least two downsides to negative ads. One, candidates must take time and energy away from promoting themselves in order to criticize opponents. For example, most candidates have limited resources to spend producing ads. Therefore, as candidates spend money on negative ads, they have fewer resources for promotional ads. Candidates on the attack, then, may experience a drop in their own evaluations for no other reason than that they are spending time talking exclusively about the opponent. Second, as we discussed earlier, there is a possibility of a voter backlash, as candidates on the offensive are viewed less favorably by voters.

We turn first to an examination of the relationship between negative information and voters' evaluations of incumbents. Every measure of negative information decreases citizens' evaluations of incumbents (see Table 5.4). Incumbents engaged in hostile and shrill campaigns can expect lower evaluations by voters. In addition, press criticisms have a strong negative influence on citizens' feelings. For example, a one-unit change in the proportion of press criticisms lowers evaluations of incumbents by nearly eleven points (i.e., 10.96) on average.[31] Thus, an incumbent in a race with little negative press commentary is far better off than an incumbent faced with constant criticisms.

In addition, assessments of incumbents decrease as the proportion of the challengers' commercials become negative. Challengers, by attacking incumbents, erode voter support of incumbent senators. In contrast, when incumbents attack challengers, voters' evaluations of the attacking incumbents become more negative. Although we cannot be certain of the reason for the decline, either backlash or lack of attention promoting their own candidacies, incumbents pay a price for launching negative ads against challengers.[32]

Turning to challengers, negative campaign information influences citizens' evaluations of challengers, but far less dramatically than of incumbents. To be sure, mudslinging produces more negative evaluations of challengers. Critical coverage in the press also produces lower evaluations of challengers, although the effect is less powerful than for incumbents. In addition, challengers are harmed when incumbents attack them in commercials. As the proportion of incumbents' ads become negative, citizens' evaluations of challengers decline.

We can draw direct comparisons between the effect of incumbents' commercials on citizens' evaluations of challengers (–2.81), and the effect of incumbents' ads on citizens' evaluations of their own candidacies (–2.95). The impact is remarkably similar. In fact, when we examine the standard errors (i.e., measures calculating the range of the effects of the incumbents' ads on the feeling thermometers), it is clear that evaluations of the challengers *and* the incumbents are equally influenced by the negativity of the incumbents' advertisements. Put simply, incumbents hurt themselves and their opponents simultaneously.

Finally, challengers do not harm their own evaluations when they attack incumbents.[33] It is possible that the public views negative campaigning by challengers as an appropriate campaign strategy against entrenched incumbents.[34] How else can challengers unseat senior incumbents? Challengers, then, are not penalized when they use negative commercials. However, if challengers overstep the bounds of civility by engaging in mudslinging, their evaluations suffer.

TABLE 5.4 HOW NEGATIVE INFORMATION INFLUENCES
CITIZENS' EVALUATIONS OF CANDIDATES

	INCUMBENTS		CHALLENGERS	
	OLS COEFFICIENTS (STANDARD ERRORS)	BETA	*OLS COEFFICIENTS (STANDARD ERRORS)*	BETA
Negative Campaign Information				
Mudslinging	−1.37 (.46)***	−.04	−1.17 (.38)***	−.04
Incumbents' Ads	−2.95 (1.38)**	−.03	−2.81 (1.14)***	−.04
Challengers' Ads	−2.43 (1.00)***	−.03	−.96 (.83)	−.02
Press Criticisms of Incumbents	−10.96 (4.82)***	−.03		
Press Criticisms of Challengers			−6.07 (3.42)*	−.02
Characteristics of the Race				
Incumbent Spending	−.41 (.30)***	−.02	−1.49 (.25)***	−.09
Challenger Spending	2.12 (.47)***	.07	2.12 (.44)***	.09
Competition	−.21 (.02)***	−.15	.06 (.02)***	.06
Open	1.35 (.96)	.02	1.81 (.67)***	.03
Characteristics of the Candidates				
Seniority	.04 (.04)	.01		
Challenger Quality			.09 (.04)**	.03
Gender	2.91 (2.07)	.02	1.81 (.67)***	.03
Political Characteristics of Citizens				
Partisanship	3.66 (.28)***	.20	1.82 (.22)***	.12
Ideology	1.05 (.16)***	.07	1.00 (.14)***	.09
Issues	1.14 (.30)***	.05	1.13 (.24)***	.06
Economic Voting	.79 (.27)***	.04	.06 (.23)	.01
Presidential Approval	1.29 (.22)***	.08	.98 (.18)***	.08
Presidential Coattails	2.68 (.66)***	.05	3.65 (.55)***	.09
Intercept	77.27 (1.74)***		44.01 (2.74)***	
N	6110		6110	
R^2	.16		.11	

***p < .01
**p < .05
*p < .10
The p-values are based on two-tailed tests.

To illustrate further the effects of negativity on citizens' evaluations, we calculate voters' assessments of incumbents and challengers in four common campaign scenarios. In each scenario we vary levels of negativity and competition because, as we demonstrated in earlier chapters, these two forces go hand-in-hand. Competition breeds negativity by candidates and in the press. The four types of races are (1) highly competitive campaigns in which both candidates are extremely negative, (2) moderately competitive campaigns in which both candidates are somewhat negative, (3) noncompetitive campaigns in which challengers are negative, and (4) noncompetitive campaigns in which both candidates refrain from negativity.[35]

Campaigns have the strongest effects on citizens' evaluations of incumbents (see Figure 5.2). In noncompetitive races where both candidates steer clear of negative messages, voters score incumbents 74 degrees on the feeling thermometer, nearly 25 degrees above the neutral ranking. Gradually, support for incumbents erodes as negativity and competition increase. For example, in moderately competitive races with moderate negativity, citizens score incumbents, on average, 59 degrees on the feeling thermometers. And in highly competitive races with a great deal of negativity and mudslinging, incumbents' scores on the feeling thermometers drop to 51 degrees, on average.

Voters' evaluations of challengers are far less responsive to competition and negativity. Citizens' scores vary six degrees (42–48 degrees), on average, across differing levels of competition and negativity. In the harshest campaign environment (i.e., polls are deadlocked and all campaign information

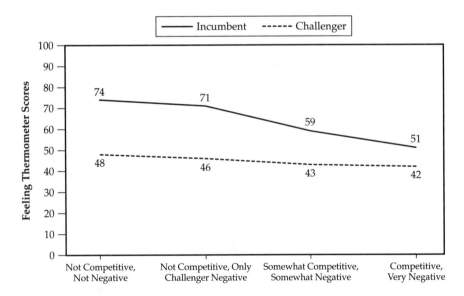

FIGURE 5.2   HOW NEGATIVITY INFLUENCES EVALUATIONS OF CANDIDATES

Source: Kahn and Kenney's data and NES/SES data. Point estimates are derived from the data in Table 5.4.

is negative), citizens score challengers, on average, 42 degrees on the feeling thermometers. Yet, a sharp contrast in the campaign setting has virtually no effect on voters' evaluations of challengers. For example, in noncompetitive campaigns in which both candidates refrain from negativity, individuals score challengers, on average, 48 degrees on the feeling thermometers.

Turning to the remaining factors in the model, we find that virtually every measure of political attitudes influences citizens' evaluations of candidates. For example, people sharing the same ideological profiles as candidates rate them significantly higher on the feeling thermometer. In addition, many of the variables measuring the characteristics of the candidates and the context of the campaign influence citizens' evaluations of the candidates. Quality challengers, for instance, are viewed more positively than their less experienced colleagues.

Summary

In general, negative campaigns affect how voters view campaigns, view candidates, and view their duties in a democracy. However, the effect of negative information varies according to its content and presentation. That is, citizens' reactions to negative information are far from uniform and vary depending on the type of negative message. Also, negative information does not affect all people in the same way. The influence of negative messages affects some people far more dramatically than others.

We explored the influence of negative campaign messages in three specific settings. First, we investigated the question: Do negative campaigns influence citizens' interest in campaigns generally? Indeed they do, but the effects vary according to the type of message. Relevant and civil critical commentary by the press generates interest among citizens. The effects of the press are quite strong, rivaling most other explanations of citizens' interest in campaigns. However, when campaigns degenerate into mudslinging, voters lose interest, literally.

Our second investigation centered on the relationship between negative campaign messages and voters' likelihood of going to the polls. Consistent with the findings for interest, the effect of negative information on turnout depends on the content and tenor of the messages. Negative critiques focusing on relevant topics and presented in an appropriate manner enhance the likelihood that citizens will vote. These messages provide distracted citizens with information to make comparisons between the candidates. In contrast, mudslinging dampens the probability that voters will go to the polls. Mean-spirited, shrill, and irrelevant messages dissuade voters from participating in the voting process. In these situations, potential voters gain little useful information and are disenchanted with both candidates.

Still further, negative messages do not affect all voters uniformly. The people least likely to vote, on any occasion, are most affected by negative campaigns. Specifically, citizens not attached to parties, citizens lacking interest in elections, citizens holding little information about politics, and citizens disadvantaged by means of race or income are affected by negative messages far more dramatically than their respective counterparts. Critical discourse about relevant topics that is presented in an appropriate manner resonates with people who rarely focus on politics and prompts them to cast ballots. This type of information provides them with reasons to support one candidate or party over another. The exact opposite is true for mudslinging. Harsh and irrelevant information acts to dissuade these voters from partaking in the political process. In a contest filled with mudslinging, the contestants become unlikable and the process untenable. It is far easier to stay home.

In contrast, the psychologically engaged and politically sophisticated citizens go to the polls, irrespective of the behavior of the candidates and the press. These individuals are not dissuaded from voting when the candidates' rhetoric gets nasty and their likelihood of voting does not increase when the amount of useful critical information escalates.

These findings have important implications for the size and make-up of the voting electorate in the United States. Turnout is currently at historically low levels and the electorate is disproportionately well-educated, well-heeled, older, civic-minded, politically astute, and psychologically engaged in politics. We find that mudslinging campaigns act to further shrink the electorate and make it even more politically elite and financially affluent. Mudslinging campaigns produce a smaller and less representative electorate.

Finally, we uncovered evidence in this chapter that negative campaign information shapes voters' evaluations of candidates. Specifically, negative messages have strong effects on citizens' evaluations of incumbents. All forms and sources of negative messages depress evaluations of incumbents. Challengers' ads, press criticisms, and mudslinging lower voters' assessments of incumbents. In addition, evaluations of incumbents suffer when they attack challengers. Incumbents have little to gain when they engage in negative campaigning.

Challengers, too, are injured by negative messages, but far less dramatically than incumbents. Mudslinging, of course, depresses evaluations of challengers. Also, incumbents can lower evaluations of challengers with negative ad attacks, but the impact of these negative advertisements is not dramatic. Furthermore, challengers experience no backlash when they attack incumbents. And press criticisms have a far less impressive effect on citizens' evaluations of challengers, compared to incumbents. Challengers, unlike incumbents, have reasons to attack incumbents. Evaluations of their own candidacies will not be damaged and they will depress citizens' views of incumbents, especially if they attack without mudslinging.

In the end, then, negative campaign messages have pervasive effects on voters' attitudes and behaviors. The effects are complex and multifaceted. They vary according to the content and tone of messages and they change in response to the characteristics of the citizens. Most succinctly, negative messages influence who votes and how voters evaluate competing candidates.

NOTES

1. For a detailed description of this race, see Clyde Wilcox, "They Did It Their Way: Campaign Finance Principles and Realities Clash in Wisconsin in 1998," in *Campaigns and Elections: Contemporary Case Studies*, ed. Michael A. Bailey, Ronald A. Faucheux, Paul S. Herrnson, and Clyde Wilcox (Washington, D.C.: Congressional Quarterly Press, 2000).
2. According to recent research—see, for example, Kenneth Goldstein's *Interest Groups, Lobbying, and Participation in America* (New York: Cambridge University Press, 1999)—groups often work to encourage higher turnout among like-minded followers.
3. M. Margaret Conway, *Political Participation in the United States*, 2nd ed. (Washington, D.C.: CQ Press, 1991).
4. William H. Flanigan and Nancy H. Zingale, *Political Behavior of the American Electorate*, 10th ed. (Washington, D.C.: CQ Press, 2002).
5. These are the same forces we used as control variables in Chapter 4 (See Appendix A). Also, for specific literature on voters' interest in campaigns, see William H. Flanigan and Nancy H. Zingale, *Political Behavior of the American Electorate*.
6. See Appendix A for information about how these variables are measured.
7. To assess the relative strength among the variables in Table 5.1 we rely on the standardized coefficients.
8. See, for example, Stephen Ansolabehere, Shanto Iyengar, Adam Simon, and Nicholas Valentine, "Does Attack Advertising Demobilize the Electorate?" *American Political Science Review* 88, no. 4 (1994): 829–838; Stephen Ansolabehere and Shanto Iyengar, *Going Negative: How Political Advertisements Shrink and Polarize the Electorate* (New York: The Free Press, 1995).
9. See Paul Freedman and Ken Goldstein, "Measuring Media Exposure and the Effects of Negative Campaign Ads," *American Journal of Political Science* 43, no. 4 (2000): 1189–1208; Steven Finkel and John Geer, "A Spot Check: Casting Doubt on the Demobilizing Effect of Attack Advertising," *American Journal of Political Science* 42, no. 2 (1998): 573–595; Kathleen Hall Jamieson, *Everything You Think You Know About Politics—and Why You're Wrong* (New York: Basic Books, 2000).
10. In particular, see Kim Fridkin Kahn and Patrick J. Kenney, "Do Negative Campaigns Mobilize or Suppress Turnout? Clarifying the Relationship between Negativity and Participation," *American Political Science Review* 93, no. 4 (1999): 877–889.
11. The 1988 presidential election was particularly negative. People may have stayed home on account of the negativity in the presidential race, thus contaminating our analyses of the senate campaigns. For a discussion of the negativity in the 1988 and 1992 presidential campaigns, see Paul R. Abramson, John H. Aldrich, and David W. Rhode, *Change and Continuity in the 1988 Elections* (Washington, D.C.: Congressional Quarterly Press, 1990); and Paul R. Abramson, John H. Aldrich, and David W. Rhode, *Change and Continuity in the 1992 Elections* (Washington, D.C.: Congressional Quarterly Press, 1995).
12. When examining the impact of negativity on turnout in 1990, we controlled for psychological factors known to influence participation (i.e., partisan attachment, interest in campaigns), attention/knowledge of the campaign (i.e., difference in evaluations of candidates, favorability toward candidates, contact with candidates, exposure to candidates, knowledge of candidates, mention of campaign theme), contextual factors (i.e., closeness of senate race, presence of gubernatorial campaign, closeness of gubernatorial campaign, tone of gubernatorial campaign, proportion of competitive House races), and demographic characteristics (i.e., education, age, income, employment status, home ownership, length of residency, residency in South). See Appendix A for information about how these variables are measured.

13. See Angus Campbell, "Surge and Decline: A Study of Electoral Change," *Public Opinion Quarterly* 24, no. 3 (1960): 397–418; Philip E. Converse, "The Concept of a Normal Vote," in *Elections and the Political Order*, ed. Angus Campbell, Philip E. Converse, Warren E. Miller, and Donald E. Stokes (New York: Wiley, 1966); V. O. Key, Jr., *American State Politics* (New York: Knopf, 1956).

14. Philip E. Converse, "Information Flow and the Stability of Partisan Attitudes," *Public Opinion Quarterly* 26, no. 4 (1962): 578–599; Philip E. Converse, "The Nature of Belief Systems in Mass Publics," in *Ideology and Discontent*, ed. David Apter (New York: Free Press, 1964); Robert Luskin, "Measuring Political Sophistication," *American Journal of Political Science* 31, no. 4 (1987): 856–899; John R. Zaller, *Nature and Origins of Mass Opinion* (Cambridge: Cambridge University Press, 1992).

15. Sidney Verba, Kay Lehman Schlozman, and Henry Brady, *Voice and Equality: Civic Voluntarism in American Politics* (Boston, MA: Harvard University Press, 1995).

16. Converse, "The Nature of Belief Systems in Mass Publics"; Warren E. Miller and J. Merrill Shanks, *The New American Voter* (Cambridge, MA: Harvard University Press, 1996).

17. Sidney Verba, Kay Lehman Schlozman, and Henry Brady, *Voice and Equality: Civic Voluntarism in American Politics* (Boston, MA: Harvard University Press, 1995).

18. Respondents were classified as *Independents* or *Partisans* based on their answer to the "root" party identification question. We relied on the political interest question to classify people as *Low in Political Interest* (respondents who said they were "somewhat interested" or "not much interested" in political campaigns) or *High in Political Interest* (respondents who said they were "very much interested" in political campaigns). We developed a measure of political sophistication to assess people's levels of political information. Based on answers to six questions available in the NES/SES, we divide respondents into two categories: *Political Novices* (respondents correctly answering zero to four of the knowledge questions) and *Political Experts* (respondents correctly answering five to six of the knowledge questions). Finally, *Minority/Poor* are African Americans, Hispanics, or people whose families made less than $20,000 a year, while *Whites/Not Poor* are whites or people whose families made $20,000 a year or more.

19. While analyzing these particular subpopulations, we controlled for all of the rival explanations of turnout presented in Appendix B.

20. See Richard D. Ashmore and Frances K. Del Boca, "Sex Stereotypes and Implicit Personality Theory: Toward a Cognitive-Social Psychological Conceptualization," *Sex Roles* 5 (1979): 219–248; David Easton and Jack Dennis, *Children in the Political System* (New York: McGraw-Hill, 1969); Diana Owen and Jack Dennis, "Gender Differences in the Politicization of American Children," *Women and Politics* 8, no. 2 (1988): 23–43.

21. We hold the rival forces discussed earlier and presented in Appendix B constant (e.g., characteristics of the race, citizen characteristics) when examining gender differences in the impact of negative messages on turnout.

22. See Gary C. Jacobson, *The Politics of Congressional Elections* (New York: Longman, 2001). All of the variables used in the analyses of citizens' evaluations are operationalized in Appendix A.

23. Peverill Squire, "Challenger Quality and Voting Behavior in U.S. Senate Elections," *Legislative Studies Quarterly* 21 (1992): 235–248; Richard F. Fenno, *Senators on the Campaign Trail* (Norman, OK: University of Oklahoma Press, 1986); Peverill Squire and Eric R. A. N. Smith, "A Further Examination of Challenger Quality in Senate Elections," *Legislative Studies Quarterly* 21 (1996): 235–248.

24. See Gary C. Jacobson, *The Politics of Congressional Elections* (New York: Longman, 2001). Also, see Gary C. Jacobson, *Money in Congressional Elections* (New Haven, CT: Yale University Press, 1980).

25. See Kim F. Kahn and Patrick J. Kenney, *The Spectacle of U.S. Senate Campaigns* (Princeton, NJ: Princeton University Press, 1999).

26. Alan I. Abramowitz and Jeffrey A. Segal, *Senate Elections* (Ann Arbor, MI: University of Michigan Press, 1992).

27. Gerald C. Wright, Jr. and Mark B. Berkman, "Candidates and Policy in U.S. Senate Elections," *American Political Science Review* 80 (1986): 567–590.

28. See Robert M. Stein, "Economic Voting for Governor and U.S. Senator: The Electoral Consequences of Federalism," *Journal of Politics* 52 (1990): 29–53.

29. See James E. Campbell and Joe A. Sumners, "Presidential Coattails in Senate Elections," *American Political Science Review* 84 (1990): 513–524.

30. See Gary C. Jacobson, *The Politics of Congressional Elections* (New York, Longman, 2001).

31. In calculating the point estimate, we hold all remaining variables in Table 5.4 at their means.

32. Incumbents, of course, are aware of this problem. They prefer to develop campaign messages that center on images highlighting their performance in office. For a full discussion of these types of positive strategies, see Paul S. Herrnson, *Congressional Elections: Campaigning at Home and in Washington*, 2nd ed. (Washington, D.C.: Congressional Quarterly Press, 1998).

33. The coefficient for the challenger ads in the model predicting the challengers' feeling thermometer score is insignificant.

34. For further discussion on this strategy see Kenneth M. Goldstein, Jonathan S. Krasno, Lee Bradford, and Daniel E. Seltz, "Going Negative: Attack Advertising in the 1998 Elections," in *Playing Hardball: Campaigning for the U.S. Congress*, ed. Paul S. Herrnson (Upper Saddle River, NJ: Prentice Hall, 2001).

35. We present the average evaluations for all citizens scoring incumbents and challengers on the feeling thermometers for each of the four campaign scenarios. For each campaign setting, we use the models presented in Table 5.4 to calculate average "point estimates" on the feeling thermometers while holding all remaining variables at their means.

6

THE IMPACT OF NEGATIVE MESSAGES: SOME ANSWERS

At the dawn of the twenty-first century, politicians, pundits, and citizens believe that negative campaigns are everywhere, regularly invading America's federal elections. Most observers contend that the candidates and the press are primarily responsible for the relentless negative contests. Listen to the frustration about contemporary campaigns.

Victor Kamber, a top Washington political consultant, in his book *Poison Politics*:

> In the past few years, American politics has been poisoned by harsh personal attacks, primarily in short television spot advertisements. Political campaigns have become increasingly negative, and attack ads on television are more prevalent and shriller in tone. The arguments have often become ridiculous, irrelevant and irresponsible.
>
> Curtis Gans of the Committee for the Study of the American Electorate: The tenor (of campaigns) is not getting worse, because that's always been bad, but it's this volume of negative advertising.
>
> E. J. Dionne, political columnist and author: Others who have considered the trends suggest that negative campaigning is worse not in its nastiness but in its broader, cumulative effects on the body politic.
>
> Richard Gephardt, Majority Leader of the U.S. House of Representatives: We're destroying a process with negative advertising, which is giving everybody a very cynical attitude about politics.
>
> David Doak, Democratic Political Consultant: There were always negative things said on the stump, but not with a thousand gross ratings points (i.e., a measure of TV audience) behind them and not in your living room while you were eating your popcorn.
>
> President Clinton in 1994: For people to be kept in constant turmoil all the time, where they don't listen to one another, they don't talk to one another, they just are bombarded by these negative ads on television, I think is not good for our democracy, and it is frankly not realistic.
>
> The feelings of over 1000 citizens in November 2000 were captured in a poll for the Pew Research Center conducted by Princeton Survey Research

Associates. Respondents were asked: "Students are often given the grades A, B, C, D, or Fail to describe the quality of their work. Looking back over the campaign (2000), what grade would you give to the press. . . ." Only six percent scored the press an A, while 32 percent gave the press D or F grades for their coverage of the 2000 campaigns. Citizens were also asked, "Thinking about the campaign again: How helpful were the candidates' commercials to you in deciding which candidate to vote for? Would you say they were very helpful, somewhat helpful, not too helpful, or not at all helpful?" Only six percent responded "very helpful" and 42 percent claimed the commercials were "not at all helpful" after the 2000 campaign. The same question was posed after the 1996 and 1992 elections, and the responses were strikingly similar.

CNN exit polls conducted after the 1998 senatorial and 2000 presidential elections consistently found that citizens thought many candidates "attacked unfairly." In fact, if the race was close, a majority of voters believed at least one candidate "attacked unfairly."

Are these claims, although typical, exaggerated? We think so. In this monograph we have marshaled evidence showing that negative campaigns are not monolithic. In actuality, negative campaigning is not predestined to occur as election day approaches. In addition, the press is not consumed with producing only negative stories. To be sure, the press print negative messages in competitive campaigns, but reporters and editors do not simply mimic the attacks of the candidates, far from it.

Our focus has been on senatorial campaigns. We explored negative messages in nearly one hundred U.S. Senate campaigns and found that wholesale negativity is not the norm.[1] Put simply, elections for the U.S. Senate are not awash in negativity. In fact, the majority of senatorial elections involve little or no negative discussion. Negative messages are present in approximately 40 percent of senate races, but only about 20 percent of senate races are intensely negative.[2] Negativity is also highly predictable; hostile attacks between candidates occur only under certain circumstances. Politicians are not bred to attack opponents reflexively.

The most surefire predictor of negative campaign discourse is competition. When polls indicate that the outcome of the race is uncertain, candidates go negative. And they do so viciously in some cases. Highly competitive races, those where polls indicate the race is a "dead heat," deteriorate quickly into mudslinging. Candidates' attacks can be shrill and are often not related directly to governing. Even when races begin in late summer or early fall with little or no negativity, if polls indicate the gap between the candidates is narrowing then, by mid-October, negative attack ads begin to dominate the airwaves.

Alongside competition, there are two other predictable correlates of negativity. One is the status of the candidate. Challengers, because they need to turn voters away from incumbents, tend to attack even when they trail in the polls. Their strategy is to provide voters with reasons to vote against incumbents. Incumbents, on the other hand, prefer to stay away from attacking their opponents until the polls suggest that the outcome of the race is uncertain. When threatened, incumbents waste no time and spare no resources to criticize challengers.

The final predictor of negativity is the calendar. Candidates tend to attack one another in the final days of campaigns. If candidates are short of resources, they wait until the end of the campaign and spend their last few dollars criticizing opponents. Attacks near the end of campaigns are difficult to refute since all advertisements stop on election day, no matter how much candidates want to have the final word.

Compared to candidates, even less negativity emanates from the press, far less. From 1988 to 1992, across fifty newspapers covering nearly one hundred U.S. Senate races, the amount of negative paragraphs, as a proportion of all paragraphs printed about a campaign, never exceeded 20 percent. On average, only about 10 percent of the coverage devoted to incumbents was negative and the percentage of negative coverage about challengers was only slightly higher. The truth is negative press coverage is almost nonexistent unless races become competitive.

Put simply, the most dramatic predictor of negative press coverage is competition. Campaigns with uncertain outcomes are interesting and dramatic and, therefore, these races garner press attention. In competitive races, the candidates are attacking one another and these attacks spill over into the press. However, the candidates do not control the topics of coverage. Try as they might, candidates are not very successful at cajoling the press to carry their attacks to opponents. For example, when challengers attack and criticize incumbents, these criticisms do not turn up in the press. Incumbents, too, are frustrated. In fact, when incumbents attack challengers, they experience a backlash in the press. For instance, attacks by incumbents generate more negative headlines for their own candidacies, and yet no additional negative headlines are printed about the challengers.

The press have begun to dissect the criticisms disseminated by the candidates' campaigns. Since the early 1990s, the press have been relying on "ad watches" to monitor the candidates' ads for accuracy and fairness in the hopes of improving the quality of campaign discourse. Not surprisingly, large numbers of the candidates' ads are found to contain inaccuracies.

The results of our study seriously challenge the conventional wisdom that the press is a major contributor to the culture of negative campaigns. The press is relatively uninterested in senatorial campaigns until they become competitive. Once outcomes are uncertain, the press begin to print negative stories, but they do not simply mirror the candidates' criticisms. It is unfair to place blame on the press for fostering negative campaign discourse in U.S. Senate elections.

UNMITIGATED CONFUSION: THE EFFECTS OF NEGATIVE CAMPAIGNS ON CITIZENS' ACTIONS AND ATTITUDES

Opinions about how negative campaigning affects civic engagement vary remarkably. Listen to the confusion:

> Former President Clinton: One of the things that concerns me about campaigns when they become too negative is that a lot of people can then just get kind of turned off and say, well maybe this doesn't have anything to do with me.
>
> Stephen Ansolabehere and Shanto Iyengar from UCLA: Our most troubling finding is that negative or attack advertising actually suppresses turnout.
>
> Kathleen Hall Jamieson: . . . we do see a clear positive relationship between advertising and voter turnout . . . contrast [advertising] is the most effective in mobilizing voters. By our definition, this is advertising with only moderate levels of attack.
>
> Douglas Schoen (a pollster for the Clinton campaign in 1996): It isn't bad for the democracy if real philosophical differences between two candidates, or two parties are aired, and I think [when campaigns] make clear statements of Democratic and Republican philosophies that may in the short term benefit democracy.

Why all the confusion? We think a great deal of the ambiguity can be clarified by considering (1) the type of negative information presented by candidates and (2) the characteristics of the voters receiving the negative information. To begin, we find that the type, tone, and content of negative information has a dramatic effect on turnout. When negative critiques focus on topics relevant to governing and are presented in a civil manner, turnout increases. Yet, when candidates attack their opponents for actions unrelated to governing or when attacks are presented in a shrill or harsh manner, turnout declines.

Furthermore, different types of people react differently to negative messages. Citizens unconnected to the political world, due either to lack of interest or resources, are most influenced by negative talk. Negative critiques are helpful for these individuals. Specifically, thoughtful and reasonable criticisms related to governing mobilize nonpartisans, politically unsophisticated individuals, and poorer citizens.

In turn, mudslinging has a particularly dampening effect on these same voters. Individuals who are uninterested in politics, who lack a reservoir of information about political events, or who lack personal and financial resources are likely to respond to mudslinging by disengaging from politics. These folks are predisposed to dislike politics and shrill and irrelevant attacks reinforce their displeasure and lead them to stay home on election day.

Thus, the confusion noted by scholars and pundits regarding the impact of negative campaigning on turnout is clarified when we consider the tenor and content of negativity as well as the characteristics of the citizens receiving the negative information.

How negative campaigns influence evaluations of candidates has also been a hotly debated topic. Listen to the views of politicians, the public, consultants, and pundits:

> David Gergen (former advisor to Presidents Nixon, Reagan, and Clinton): Negative campaigns tend to be very, very polarizing. They discourage voters, they make the voter feel manipulated and belittled and it leaves the person who wins with an inability to really unify the country behind important national goals.
>
> Dan Romer, Kathleen Hall Jamieson, and Joseph Cappella (Annenberg School of Communication at the University of Pennsylvania): . . . differences in advertising between the candidates produced differential effects on vote share. Advocacy ads were the strongest force for voter share, followed by contrast ads. Attack ads appeared to backfire on the candidate who sponsored them by producing a small but detectable decline in vote share.
>
> Richard Lau and Gerald Pomper: We ask a simple question: how effective is negative campaigning in helping to get candidates elected? Our results provide no straightforward answer. Generally speaking, but dependent on the opponent's strategy, negative campaigning is relatively effective for challengers, while positive campaigning is more effective for incumbents.

We think we bring some clarity to this confusion as well. As before, it is necessary to consider the nature of the attack: the substance and tenor of the criticisms. In addition, we need to consider who is making the attack: the incumbent or the challenger. When we take into account these two factors, the relationship between negative campaigning and citizens' evaluations of candidates becomes far less perplexing. First, we find that mudslinging hurts all candidates' evaluations. When the campaign environment degenerates into attacks that are uncivil and unrelated to governing, impressions of both incumbents and challengers become more negative. Mudslinging depresses citizens' views of the competing candidates, even controlling for a host of forces known to explain evaluations, such as citizens' partisanship and ideology.

In addition, considering the source of the attack moves us a step closer to understanding the dynamics of negative campaigns. Incumbents reap few benefits when they attack. While incumbents are able to lower voters' evaluations of challengers, they pay a price. Citizens develop less favorable impressions of incumbents who attack their opponents.

We know incumbents typically shy away from negative attacks until polls suggest the race is competitive. However, incumbents begin to fight back as soon as they believe their jobs are in jeopardy. At this point, incumbents and their strategists face a dilemma. They must defend themselves against an aggressive challenger, all the while knowing that their own evaluations are going to suffer. Once the duel becomes negative, incumbents must refrain from mudslinging because their evaluations will drop even more dramatically.

The story for challengers is more straightforward. When challengers attack incumbents, evaluations of incumbents drop, but their own evaluations are unchanged. Challengers do not experience a backlash when they mount an offensive against incumbents. The public appears to accept the idea that challengers must attack incumbents in order to make a case for their own candidacies. After all, incumbents are elected officials who have represented the public for years. It is altogether appropriate for challengers to raise questions about the senators' stewardship, as long as the criticisms are civil and relevant.

So, knowing the tone, content, and source of negative messages helps us clarify the relationship between negative campaigning and evaluations of the candidates. Citizens' reactions to negative campaigning are quite reasonable. Americans do not like mudslinging and they will punish candidates who engage in attacks viewed as unworthy of public discourse. Furthermore, appropriate attacks by challengers are considered acceptable by voters, maybe even necessary, and have the desired effect of lowering evaluations of incumbents. Finally, criticisms offered by incumbents are seen as less acceptable. While these criticisms hurt citizens' impressions of challengers, they also depress citizens' evaluations of the incumbents.

In the end, elections are the primary forum for discussions between citizens and politicians in the United States. Only during elections do large numbers of candidates go before large numbers of citizens and discuss the state of the nation and its future. The quality of these discussions is important for nurturing citizens' connections with their representatives in the short run; but these discussions are equally vital for establishing and maintaining citizens' support of America's democratic experiment in the long run. It is vital, then, for politicians, the press, scholars, and citizens to come to grips with how negative campaigns affect the quality of democratic elections.

NOTES

1. We realize that a great many people form impressions about negative campaigns from the presidential contests. Although presidential campaigns are replete with negative messages that trickle down to millions of citizens, recent evidence suggests that presidential campaigns are not as negative as citizens believe, nor was the 2000 presidential election as negative as the 1996 and 1992 campaigns. See Kathleen Hall Jamieson, *Everything You Think You Know About Politics—and Why You're Wrong* (New York: Basic Books, 2000).
2. The amount of negativity in U.S. House races is even lower. See Paul Herrnson, *Congressional Elections: Campaigning at Home and in Washington* (Washington, D.C.: CQ Press, 1998).

A

MEASUREMENT APPENDIX

CHARACTERISTICS OF THE CANDIDATES

CHALLENGER QUALITY

This measure is based on the challenger's experience and the challenger's campaign skills. Challenger experience is based on a nine-point scale: 9 = sitting governor, 8 = House members and statewide officials serving more than one term, 7 = first-term House members and first-term statewide officials, 6 = mayors of major cities, 5 = state legislative leaders, 4 = state legislators, 3 = other local office holders, 2 = celebrities, 1 = non-celebrities. The candidates' campaign skills are based on descriptions in the *CQ Weekly Report* and the *Almanac of American Politics*. Candidates described as skillful campaigners are scored 3, candidates with a mixture of positive and negative reports are scored 2, and candidates described as poor campaigners receive a score of 1. The experience measure is multiplied with the skill measure to create the measure of challenger quality.

GENDER

This variable is coded as a binary where 1 = female; 0 = male.

SENIORITY

Years in office.

CHARACTERISTICS OF CITIZENS

AGE

This is an interval variable ranging from 18 to 97. In estimating the impact of age, we also included a first-order polynomial (i.e., age^2) to pick up the curvilinear relationship between age and turnout.

Attention to the News

This measure was based on the following question: "How many days in the past week did you watch news programs on TV?" and "How many days in the past week did you read a daily newspaper?" We created an index ranging from zero to 14, with a score of 14 representing an individual who reported reading a newspaper every day and watching a news program every day. Zero indicates that an individual reported never reading the paper or watching a news program.

Contact with Candidates

The following five items from the NES/SES survey were used to assess personal contact: met with the candidate, attended a meeting where the candidate spoke, talked to a member of the candidate's staff, received mail from the candidate, and knew someone who had contact with the candidate. We created an index ranging from 0 (i.e., an individual reports no contact with the candidate) to five (i.e., a respondent reports contact with the candidate in all five situations).

Education

This is an interval measure based on the question, "What is the highest grade of school or year of college you have completed?"

Interest

This measure is based on the NES/SES question, "Some people don't pay much attention to political campaigns. How about you? Would you say that you are very much interested, somewhat interested, or not much interested?"

Knowledge of the Candidates

This variable is a three-point measure to assess a respondent's ability to recognize and recall the candidates' names. Citizens who can recall *and* recognize both candidates' names were scored 2; citizens who accomplished only one of these tasks received a score of 1; citizens who were unable to recall or recognize either candidate were scored 0.

Favorability toward Candidates

Respondents who rated both candidates positively (i.e., greater than 50 on the feeling thermometer) were coded 2; citizens who rated one candidate positively were coded 1; and citizens who rated neither candidate positively were coded 0.

INCOME

We measured income on a six-point scale ranging from 1 (less than $10,000) to 6 ($60,000 or more).

HOME OWNERSHIP

This is a binary variable where respondents who report owning their own homes were coded 1, otherwise respondents received a code of 0.

LENGTH OF RESIDENCE

This is an interval scale based on years at current residence.

MENTION CAMPAIGN THEME

The NES/SES asked respondents the following question: "In your state, what issue did the candidates talk about most during the campaign for the Senate?" Respondents who answered the question received a score of 1, individuals who did not answer the question received a score of 0.

STRENGTH OF PARTY ATTACHMENT

The standard NES/SES seven-point party identification question was recoded into four categories: independents were coded 0; leaning partisans were coded 1; weak partisans were coded 2; and strong partisans were coded 3.

SOPHISTICATION

This measure is based on six NES/SES question: (1) "correct" placements of George Bush; and correct placements of the (2) Democratic and (3) Republican parties on the seven-point liberal/conservative continuum. Respondents' answers were coded correct if they said George Bush or the Republican party was moderate to extremely conservative. Similarly, respondents' answers were coded correct if they said the Democratic party was moderate to extremely liberal. We also measured respondents' levels of information about the senator not up for reelection in the state, since information about the senator seeking reelection is contaminated by the ongoing campaign. We utilize the following three NES/SES measures to assess knowledge of the senator not seeking re-election: (4) correct recognition of the senator's name; (5) correct recall of the senator's name; (6) correct ideological placement of the senator. To measure correct ideological placement, we recoded ADA scores to range from 1 to 3 (1 = liberal, 2 = moderate, 3 = conservative) and averaged the scores for the two years prior to the respondent's interview date. Each respondent's answer to the ideological placement of the senator was also recoded from 1 to 3 (1 = liberal, 2 = moderate, 3 = conservative). If the difference between the respondent's recoded score and the recoded ADA score was 0, the respondent correctly identified the ideological placement of the senator. If the score was different from 0, the respondent incorrectly identified the ideological placement of the senator.

CHARACTERISTICS OF THE RACE

CAMPAIGN SPENDING

Spending for both candidates was logged to base 10 and divided by the state's voting age population.

COMPETITION

We calculated difference in support of the candidates in preelection polls from 100, creating a scale ranging from 24 in the least competitive (100 − 76 = 24) to 100 in the most competitive race (100 − 0 = 100).

OPEN RACE

Incumbent races were coded 1 and open races were coded 0.

WEEK OF CAMPAIGN

This measure divided the days of the campaign into three periods: September 1 through September 24 was coded 1; September 25 through October 13 was coded 2; October 14 through election day was coded 3.

CITIZENS' ATTITUDES AND BEHAVIOR

CITIZENS' EVALUATIONS OF CANDIDATES

The standard NES/SES feeling thermometer question was used to assess citizens' views of the candidates. Respondents were asked: "I'll read the name of a person and I'd like you to rate that person using something called the feeling thermometer. You can choose any number between 0 and 100. The higher the number, the warmer or more favorable you feel toward that person; the lower the number, the colder or less favorable. You would rate the person at the 50 degree mark if you feel neither warm nor cold toward them."

TURNOUT

Respondents were asked by the NES/SES: "Did you vote for a candidate for the U.S. Senate?" Respondents who answered "yes," were coded 1, otherwise respondents were coded 0. Unfortunately, validated vote is not available in the NES/SES.

CITIZENS' KNOWLEDGE OF CAMPAIGN

EXPOSURE

The NES/SES asked respondents if they remembered seeing the candidates on television, remembered reading about the candidates in the newspaper, or recalled hearing about the candidates on the radio. We created an index ranging from 0 (i.e., respondents did not report exposure to the candidate across the three media) to 3 (i.e., respondents recall seeing the candidate on television, hearing about the candidate on the radio, and reading about the candidate in the newspaper).

IDENTIFICATION OF CORRECT THEME

The NES/SES asked respondents: "In your state, what issue did the candidates talk about the most during the campaign for the Senate?" Respondents were scored 1 if they identified the candidates' main themes; otherwise respondents received a code of 0. We used the campaign manager survey to identify the candidates' main themes because all managers were asked to identify the main themes of their campaigns.

IDENTIFICATION OF NEGATIVE THEME

This measure is based on answers to the following NES/SES question: "In your state, what issue did the candidates talk about the most during the campaign for the Senate?" Respondents who identified a negative theme were coded 1, otherwise respondents received a score of 0.

RESIDENCY IN THE SOUTH

Respondents living in states of the Old Confederacy were coded 1 (i.e., Alabama, Arkansas, Florida, Georgia, Louisiana, Mississippi, North Carolina, South Carolina, Tennessee, Texas, and Virginia); otherwise respondents received a code of 0.

WILLINGNESS TO RATE THE CANDIDATES

Respondents who rated a candidate on the "feeling thermometer" were scored a 1 (i.e., any point on the thermometer ranging from 0 to 100); otherwise respondents were scored 0.

NEGATIVITY DURING CAMPAIGNS

CANDIDATE NEGATIVITY

We employed *Congressional Quarterly* preelection assessments of the campaigns and candidates to determine if candidates were using negative campaigning.

MUDSLINGING

We relied on responses to the campaign manager survey to identify "mud-slinging" campaigns. The question posed to managers was: "What are the main themes of your opponent's campaign." If neither manager described the opponent as engaging in "mudslinging," the race received a score of 0; if one manager described the opponent as engaging in "mudslinging," the race received a score of 1; if both candidates viewed their opponent as having run a "mudslinging" campaign, the race received a score of 2.

NEGATIVITY OF CANDIDATES' ADS

The number of negative advertisements aired by each candidate divided by the total number of advertisements aired by that candidate.

PRESS CRITICISMS OF CANDIDATES

The number of critical paragraphs written about each candidate divided by the total number of paragraphs published about that candidate.

POLITICAL CHARACTERISTICS OF CITIZENS

ECONOMIC VOTING

To measure economic voting, we used the NES/SES questions: "Now, think-ing about the country as a whole, would you say that over the past year, the nation's economy has gotten better, stayed about the same, or gotten worse?" We use a five-point scale ranging from +2 (e.g., the nation's economy is much better and the incumbent is a Republican; the nation's economy is much worse and the incumbent is a Democrat) to –2 (e.g., the nation's economy is much better and the incumbent is a Democrat; the nation's economy is much worse and the incumbent is a Republican).

IDEOLOGY

To measure the impact of ideological placement on evaluations of the senate candidates, we constructed a variable capturing the "comparative ideological distances" between the respondent and the two candidates. We calculate the absolute distance between respondents' self-placement on the ideological scale and their placement of the incumbent and the challenger. Next, the respon-dents' distance from the challenger was subtracted from their distance from the incumbent. The resulting figure indicates which candidate the individual feels closer to ideologically. Respondents who do not answer the ideological questions are recoded to the middle of the scale so as not to lose them from the analysis. The final ideological score ranges from 5 (the respondent and the incumbent share the same ideological label) to –5 (the respondent and the challenger share the same ideological label).

ISSUES

The issue scale is based on respondents' spending preferences for six federal programs (i.e., the environment, education, welfare, health care, child care, and defense). The candidates' positions on the six issues were estimated by calculating a mean position for all Democratic candidates and a mean position for all Republican candidates, based on descriptions of the candidates' positions in the press. The respondents' positions were matched with the candidates' positions on each of the issues. The scale was then recoded so respondents who held identical positions with the incumbent were given the highest score, respondents sharing all the same positions as the challenger were given the lowest score. We adopted this measure because the NES/SES does not ask respondents to place candidates on issue scales.

PARTISANSHIP

The standard seven-point party identification scale is used to measure the impact of party identification on evaluations of the senate candidates. We recode party identification so that respondents who strongly identify with the party of the incumbent are given the highest score (+3), while respondents who strongly identify with the party of the challenger are given the lowest score (–3).

PRESIDENTIAL APPROVAL

The presidential approval scale ranges from +2 (e.g., the senator running for reelection is a Republican and the respondent strongly approves of the Republican president's performance; the senator running for reelection is a Democrat and the respondent strongly disapproves of the Republican president's performance) to –2 (e.g., the senator running for reelection is a Republican and the respondent strongly disapproves of the Republican president's performance; the senator running for reelection is a Democrat and the respondent strongly approves of the Republican president's performance).

PRESIDENTIAL COATTAILS

We included a measure of presidential vote choice to capture coattail voting. The coattail variable ranges from 1 (i.e., the respondent votes for a Republican for president and a Republican incumbent for Senate; the respondent votes for a Democrat for president and a Democratic incumbent for Senate) to –1 (i.e., the respondent votes for a Republican for president and a Democratic incumbent for Senate; the respondent votes for a Democrat for president and a Republican incumbent for Senate).

POLITICAL CONTEXT

CLOSENESS OF GUBERNATORIAL CAMPAIGN

The final vote tally was used to measure the competitiveness of the gubernatorial race.

COMPETITIVENESS OF U.S. HOUSE RACES

We calculated the proportion of House races in the state where the winner garnered 55 percent or less of the vote.

TONE OF THE GUBERNATORIAL CAMPAIGN

The newspapers that were content analyzed for the senate campaigns were used to assess the tone of the concurrent gubernatorial campaign. Headlines and stories about the gubernatorial race were examined if they appeared on the front page and the first page of the "state and local" section of the newspaper. Based on this content analysis, gubernatorial campaigns were scored on a four-point scale, ranging from: (1) extremely negative to (4) extremely positive.

PRESENCE OF GUBERNATORIAL CAMPAIGN

U.S. Senate elections that were concurrent with gubernatorial campaigns were scored 1; otherwise 0.

PRESIDENTIAL YEAR

We used a binary variable where 1 = presidential year; 0 = otherwise.

SIZE OF THE NEWSPAPER

We measured the number of column inches devoted to news for each newspaper.

TONE OF NEWS COVERAGE

TONE OF COVERAGE

The average tone score for all articles mainly about the candidate during the campaign.

TONE OF HEADLINE COVERAGE

The average tone score for all headlines mentioning the candidate during the campaign.

TONE OF HORSE-RACE COVERAGE

The average viability score based on all of the articles written about the candidate.

TONE OF TRAIT COVERAGE

The number of negative traits published about the candidate during the campaign.

B

How the Tenor of Campaigns
Influences Turnout

Logit Model Examining Participation in the 1990 Senate Elections

Independent Variables	Unstandardized Logit Coefficient (Standard Error)	Beta
Mudslinging	−.07 (.03)*	−.15
Tone of Campaign		
Tone of Commercials	.12 (.06)*	.15
Tone of News Coverage	2.14 (1.06)*	.18
Closeness of Senate Campaign	−.0006 (.002)	−.02
Other Campaigns		
Presence of Gubernatorial Campaign	.22 (.13)	.19
Closeness of Gubernatorial Campaign	.02 (.03)	.08
Tone of Gubernatorial Campaign	−.002 (.05)	.005
Proportion of Competitive House Races	.10 (.09)	.07
Senate Attention/Evaluation		
Difference in Evaluation of Candidates	.004 (.001)**	.19
Favorability toward Candidates	.11 (.05)*	.14
Contact with Incumbent/Open Winner	.15 (.03)**	.43
Contact with Challenger/Open Loser	.09 (.04)*	.20
Exposure to Incumbent/Open Winner	.05 (.04)	.08
Exposure to Challenger/Open Loser	−.03 (.03)	−.07
Knowledge of Incumbent/Open Winner	.18 (.06)**	.21
Knowledge of Challenger/Open Loser	.10 (.05)*	.15
Mention Campaign Theme	.16 (.06)**	.16

Independent Variables	Unstandardized Logit Coefficient (Standard Error)	Beta
Demographic Characteristics		
Educational Background	.05 (.01)**	.29
Age	.05 (.009)**	1.7
Age^2	−.0003 (.0001)**	−1.2
Income	.02 (.02)	.06
Employment Status	−.008 (.15)	.003
Home Ownership	.16(.07)*	.14
Length of Residency	.002 (.001)*	.12
Residency in the South	−.09 (.08)	.07
Psychological Involvement		
Partisan Attachment	.12 (.03)**	.25
Interest in Campaigns	.18 (.02)**	.55
Intercept	−2.97 (.36)**	

N = 2256

% of Cases Correctly Predicted = 78

Note: The p-values are based on two-tailed tests.

**p < .01

*p < .05

Source: "Do Negative Campaigns Mobilize or Suppress Turnout?" *American Political Science Review* 93, no. 4 (December 1999): 884.

INDEX